FLAVORS OF THE
SOUTHWEST
A COLLECTION OF TREASURED RECIPES

BY DOROTHY K. HILBURN

Front cover: A Southwestern Thanksgiving. PHOTO BY RICHARD EMBERY. Background, front and back cover: Arizona barrel cactus with fruit. PHOTO BY FRED HIRSCHMANN. Back cover: Fresh Ingredients. PHOTO BY CAMELBACK DESIGN GROUP, INC.

Designed by Camelback Group, Inc., 8655 E.Via de Ventura, G200, Scottsdale, AZ 85258. Telephone: 602-948-4233. Fax: 602-483-8430. Distributed by Canyonlands Publications, 4860 N. Ken Morey Drive, P.O. Box 16175, Bellemont, Arizona 86015. For ordering information call 1-520-779-3888.

Requests for additional information should be made to Camelback/Canyonlands Venture at the address above, or call our toll free telephone number: 1-800-284-6539.

Library of Congress Catalog Card Number: 94-67149
ISBN Number: 1-879924-20-X

TABLE OF CONTENTS

INTRODUCTION

Welcome to *Flavors of the Southwest*. This companion
to my earlier work, *Mexican Delights* and *Southwest Delights,*
has been a true labor of love. Most of my life has been spent in
the Southwest, with plenty of time spent in its finest kitchens
and most creative restaurants. Food, always my favorite
subject, is undoubtedly a common denominator
among people. Everyone I've met through the
development and research of these books has
shown such enthusiasm for my projects that I've
come to realize that food is not only sustenance
for our bodies but also for our hearts and souls as
well. Cooking brings people together in many ways,
and everywhere people are eager to share their favorite
recipes and cooking tips. I've tried to include as many as
relevant ones as possible in this book. I've discovered that
food opens doors, as well as hearts, and in the Southwest the
people are more than willing to share both. Many people don't
understand the essence of Southwest cooking. To some, it is
simply 'Nouvelle' Mexican, or a style in food presentation. In
some ways this is true. However, I believe true Southwestern
cooking combines both the old and the new. As new people
immigrate to the Southwest they bring their own regional
and uniquely personal styles of cooking and combine them
with flavors of Texas, New Mexico and Arizona to create
new and exciting tastes and textures, a Southwestern
style of eating. Southwest cooking has its roots in
Mexican and Native American cooking. Indians
of historic Mexico and the Southwestern
United States lived on many of the same
foods still prepared in Southwestern
kitchens today. Wild corn was first
cultivated in Mexico thousands of years
ago and is still a very important ingredient.
Foods available to the prehistoric Indians of
the Southwest were potatoes, avocados, turkey,
chiles, peanuts, beans, sweet potatoes, squash, cocoa,
pumpkins, vanilla, melons, pineapples and tomatoes.
Many recipes in this book utilize these same foods.

Settled by Spaniards, **New Mexico**
is and has always been at the forefront
of Southwestern cuisine. New Mexico is known
for its many varieties of chiles, from the hottest chiles
grown to the more decorative chile ristras, sold all over the
Southwest. Chiles from the ristras can be used in sauces
or ground to a powder for use in many Southwestern
dishes. Known for its famous art colony and an
outstanding selection of Southwestern foods,
Santa Fe has brought about a renewed
popularity of blue cornmeal,
a ritualistic grain still used
by Native Americans.

The **Texan** influence in Southwestern
cooking comes from the cowboys who tended
herds of cattle and cooked along the trail. Although no
one is exactly sure where the first bowl of chili was created,
it is commonly believed to have been the invention of a trail
cook from Texas. There are chili competitions throughout the
United States, and internationally, to determine who makes
the very best bowl of chili. Arguments abound over whether
or not beans should be included on the list of ingredients.
Purists believe that only meat, onions and spices make
up a "real" bowl of chili. Many others, myself included,
believe that the addition of other favorite foods
can only make a good thing better. Fajitas
and nachos are other Texan creations
which are popular in restaurants
throughout the Southwest.

Many of Arizona's contribution to the Southwestern style
of food preparation originate from their Mexican neighbors.
However, an influx of new cooks from across America and Europe
is constantly changing the flavors of Arizona cooking. There are
today many new cooks practicing innovative techniques in food
preparation and presentation who are bringing new attention
to Arizona's traditional cooking and food presentation styles.

HELPFUL HINTS

Use **all-purpose flour**, unless otherwise specified.

In this book we make references to **chiles** and **chili**.
Chiles are hot peppers while **chili** is a stew-like dish
and **chili powder** consists of a blend of ground
chiles mixed with several other seasonings.

Always store **fresh chiles** in a bag in the refrigerator or
string by the stems and hang to dry in a dry cool place.

All **squash blossoms** are edible. Zucchini blossoms are the
most often used in Southwestern recipes and can usually be
found in gourmet grocery stores during summer months.

Tomatillos are small, green tomato-like vegetables with an
outer papery husk, if unavailable, use green tomatoes.

❋ ❋ ❋ ❋ ❋

COMMONLY USED CHILES

Jalapeño chiles are small, dark green or yellow
chiles with a fiery flavor.

Chipotle chiles are smoked and dried Jalapeño's
that have a smoky flavor and are very hot.

California chiles, also called **Anaheim chiles**,
are long green chiles with a mild flavor.
Available in cans, either whole or chopped.

Serrano chiles are very small, green, thin and
very
hot, usually hotter that jalapeño chiles.

Poblano chiles, also called **Anchos** before being
dried, are large and dark green with a mild to hot
flavor. Poblanos are often used to make Chile Relleno.

Chile pequin is made from tiny yellow and green peppers
that, when dried and crushed, can be very hot. Use carefully!

❋ ❋ ❋ ❋ ❋

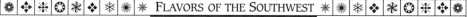
SNACKS AND APPETIZERS
SOUTHWESTERN STARTERS

Many foods eaten by early inhabitants of the Southwest are still prepared and presented today. Tortillas, beans and chiles are still the staple foods of the Southwest and when they are combined with tomatoes, cheeses, garlic and onions they create a never ending selection of dishes. Appetizers are a perfect example of how these basic foods can often be utilized to create a satisfying food finale. Many dishes that may begin as appetizers can often be served, in larger portions, as delicious main meals. In this chapter we offer the usual tasty traditional tid-bits as well as introduce several new Southwestern favorites.

✳ ✳ ✳ ✳ ✳

SHRIMP CAKES AND CHILES

INGREDIENTS:

5 medium potatoes
1/4 cup evaporated milk
1 1/2 tablespoons chili powder
1/8 teaspoon garlic powder
2 tablespoons flour
1/4 cup corn oil
1 4 ounce package dried
shrimp, powdered
1 1/2 cups water
2 eggs, beaten
Salt
Pepper

Boil potatoes until tender. Peel and mash. Add evaporated milk, flour and beaten eggs. Mix in salt and pepper to taste. Stir mixture until smooth. Add powdered shrimp and stir until mixture can be formed into small patties. Fry patties in oil until lightly brown. Set aside. Combine oil, garlic, water, flour and chili powder. Simmer over medium heat for 15 minutes, until sauce is smooth and thick, stirring often. Dip the fried patties in sauce and place on a large dish. Pour remaining hot sauce over patties.
Serves 6.

GUACAMOLE

A perennial favorite of Norte-Americanos and Mexicans,
Guacamole is the world's most popular Avocado dip.

INGREDIENTS:

2 ripe avocados
Juice from 1/2 lemon
1/2 onion, peeled and minced
1/4 teaspoon garlic powder
1/2 teaspoon chili powder
1/4 teaspoon salt
1 teaspoon Worcestershire sauce
1/2 tomato, diced

Scoop out flesh from the avocados and mash with a fork.
Mix in lemon juice. Add onion, garlic and chili powders, salt,
Worcestershire sauce and tomato and mix lightly. Chill and
serve with corn chips. Makes 2 1/2 to 3 cups. Garnish
serving dish with parsley, green onions or chiles.
Serves 6.

❋ ❋ ❋ ❋ ❋

SALSA A LA SUE

Refrigerating Salsa overnight will allow flavors time to
blend thoroughly, which creates an even better taste.

INGREDIENTS:

1 16 oz can chopped tomatoes
2 4 oz cans of green chiles
1 bunch green onions, chopped
2 beef bouillon cubes
1/2 teaspoon cumin
1/2 teaspoon garlic powder
Salt and pepper

Combine chopped tomatoes, green chiles, onions, bouillon
cubes, cumin, garlic powder and salt and pepper to taste.
Mix well and chill for at least one hour before serving.

❋ ❋ ❋ ❋ ❋

STUFFED MUSHROOMS

This sophisticated appetizer is considered a staple at many parties
and is always appreciated by mushroom lovers everywhere.

INGREDIENTS:

1 medium onion, minced
1 clove garlic, minced
2 pounds mushrooms, minced
40 large mushroom caps
4 tablespoons butter
1 1/2 cups breadcrumbs
1 cup Romano cheese, grated
Salt and pepper

Preheat oven to 450°F. In a medium pan, sauté onion, garlic and
minced mushrooms in butter. Combine breadcrumbs, Romano cheese
and salt and pepper to taste. Let cool. Rinse mushroom caps and let
dry. Fill mushrooms with onion mixture then top with the Romano
cheese and breadcrumbs. Bake for 10 minutes and serve warm.
Makes 40.

✳ ✳ ✳ ✳ ✳

NACHOS

The ultimate finger food, Nachos are an excellent way
to use leftovers. Add shrimp or crab for a seafood twist.

INGREDIENTS:

1 package tortilla chips
1/2 cup sliced jalapeño chiles
1/2 lb Monterey cheese, grated
1/2 lb Cheddar cheese, grated

On a large baking sheet place a layer of tortilla chips, covering
the pan completely. Spread shredded cheese and sliced jalapeño chiles
over corn chips and add another layer of chips. Spread cheese and
chiles over top and place under broiler until cheese melts.

✳ ✳ ✳ ✳ ✳

SCALLOP CEVICHE

Ceviche is a traditional Mexican dish and is often served
as either an appetizer or a delightfully light lunch.

INGREDIENTS:

1/2 pound scallops
Juice from 1 lemon
Juice from 1 lime
1/4 red onion, minced
1 plum tomato, diced
1 jalapeño pepper, minced
1 serrano chile pepper, minced
1/2 cup cilantro, chopped
1 green onion, chopped
1 teaspoon ketchup
1/2 teaspoon rice wine vinegar
1/8 teaspoon cayenne pepper
1/8 teaspoon pepper
Salt to taste

Combine scallops, lemon and lime juice, red onion, plum tomato,
jalapeño pepper, serrano chile pepper, cilantro, green onion, ketchup,
rice wine vinegar, cayenne pepper, black pepper and salt to
taste. Mix well and refrigerate for at least 4 hours, or overnight.
Serves 5.

✳ ✳ ✳ ✳ ✳

ROASTED PIÑON NUTS

Roasted piñon, or pine nuts, make a perfect snack
and a tasty topping for salads and soups.

INGREDIENTS:

1 pound raw piñon nuts

Spread raw, shelled piñon nuts evenly in a shallow baking
pan. Roast in oven at 300°F for one hour. Stir frequently to
brown nuts evenly. Salt nuts if desired. Serve as a snack.

✳ ✳ ✳ ✳ ✳

POTATO OMELET

This is a traditional Spanish dish that is served
as *Tapas* (a spicy finger food). Serve with or
without a sauce on the side.

INGREDIENTS:

4 large potatoes, peeled
and sliced very thin
4 eggs
1 large onion, sliced thin
1 cup olive oil
1 tablespoon parsley, chopped
2 tablespoons chopped pimentos
Salt and pepper

Preheat oven to 325°F. Using a non-stick skillet, heat the
oil and add potatoes, one slice at a time. After each layer of
potatoes add a layer of onions and salt and pepper. Cook over
low heat, turning the potatoes often, do not allow to brown.
Place cooked potatoes in a colander to drain oil.
Reserve 3 tablespoons of oil. In a large bowl, beat eggs until
foamy and add salt, parsley, pimentos and potatoes. Make sure
potatoes are covered by the egg mixture. Set mixture aside to soak
for 15 minutes. In a non-stick, oven-proof skillet, heat reserved
oil. When the oil begins to smoke, add the potato mixture,
spreading evenly over the bottom of the pan. Lower the
heat and continue to cook for 4 more minutes. Transfer the
skillet to the oven and cook for 20 minutes, or until the top
becomes a golden brown. Omelet should be firm to the touch.
Place omelet on a platter and let cool. Cut into slices and
serve at room temperature.

A WORD ABOUT SNACKS:

To make interesting new flavors of popcorn that are low
in fat and high in flavor, sprinkle chili powder, brewers
yeast or cayenne pepper over freshly popped corn.

✳ ✳ ✳ ✳ ✳

SHRIMP DIABLO

Make this great appetizer the day before your event to
give you additional time to prepare other preparations.

INGREDIENTS:

1/2 cup dry white wine
1/2 cup wine vinegar
2 tablespoons mustard
1 teaspoon horseradish
1 1/2 teaspoons paprika
1/2 teaspoon cayenne pepper
2 tablespoons ketchup
1/4 teaspoon garlic powder
1 cup vegetable oil
1 pound cooked shrimp
1/2 teaspoon salt
1 red or yellow bell pepper, sliced

In a large mixing bowl, combine white wine, vinegar, ketchup,
mustard, horseradish, garlic powder, cayenne pepper, paprika, oil
and salt. Beat ingredients until blended. Add shrimp to marinade
and let sit for at least 3 hours in refrigerator. Drain shrimp and
serve with pepper slices. Serves 6.

CON QUESO

INGREDIENTS:

1 2 lb package Velveeta cheese,
cut into large chunks
1 bunch scallions, chopped
6 medium tomatoes, chopped
1 7-3/4 oz can El Pato tomato sauce
(Mexican hot style)
1 bag tortilla chips

In a crock pot, combine Velveeta, scallions, tomatoes and
chile sauce. Cook on high heat until cheese melts. When cheese
has melted, lower heat and serve with tortilla chips.

QUESADILLAS

These simple cheese turnovers are the perfect appetizer
when served with guacamole and salsa.

INGREDIENTS:

6 flour tortillas
4 ozs Cheddar or Longhorn
cheese, shredded
1/2 teaspoon black pepper
4 ozs Monterey Jack
cheese, shredded
1 4 oz can green chiles, diced
1 cup salsa

Preheat oven to 350°F. Spray a baking sheet with non-stick
spray and cover with tortillas in a layer. Toss the cheeses together
in a small bowl and sprinkle over tortillas. Season with pepper.
Bake in oven until cheeses are melted. Sprinkle generously with
green chiles and fold in half. Dip into a favorite salsa.
Makes 6 Quesadillas.

✳ ✳ ✳ ✳ ✳

GREEN CHILE DIP

A colorful and flavorful, but mild, chile and avocado dip
that goes well with fresh vegetables and tortilla chips.

INGREDIENTS:

1 4 oz can of green chiles,
drained and chopped
1 avocado, diced
1 cup sour cream
1/2 teaspoon salt
1/2 teaspoon Tabasco sauce

Mix chiles, avocado, salt and Tabasco sauce in sour
cream. Chill for 1 hour and serve with carrot or celery
sticks or tortilla chips.
Serves 8.

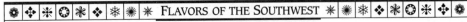
SHRIMP DIP

A creamy dip with a subtle flavor, always a
favorite at any family get-together.

INGREDIENTS:

1/4 cup chili sauce
1 teaspoon horseradish
2 teaspoons lemon juice
1/4 teaspoon hot-pepper sauce
1 cup sour cream
1 4 oz can shrimp, drained
and chopped
Salt and pepper

Mix chili sauce, horseradish, lemon juice, dash of salt and pepper
and hot-pepper sauce. Fold in sour cream and chopped shrimp.
Chill for one hour and serve with corn chips or sliced vegetables.
Makes 1 3/4 cups.

CHEESE CRISP

These cheese crisps are a simple but filling snack. Serve with
salsa, sour cream, a dash of Tabasco sauce and guacamole
on the side to make a light meal.

INGREDIENTS:

1 large flour tortilla
1 tablespoon crushed red peppers
1/2 cup Cheddar cheese,
grated

Place tortilla on a flat baking sheet and sprinkle cheese evenly
over the top. Bake under medium heat, about 350°F, until cheese
is completely melted. Sprinkle with crushed red peppers.
Serves 2.

* * * * *

SWEET PEPPER BALLS

INGREDIENTS:

2 pounds beef, boiled
2 pounds pork, boiled
2 7 oz cans green chiles,
drained and chopped
1 large sweet onion, diced
2 eggs
1/2 cup sugar
1/2 cup raisins
1/2 cup walnuts,
chopped fine
1/2 cup flour
2/3 cup shortening

Boil meat until cooked thoroughly. Put the cooled meat through a meat grinder. Cook onions and add the ground meat, chiles, sugar, raisins and walnuts and stir to mix well. Set aside to cool. Separate egg whites and yolks. Beat whites until they become quite stiff then fold in beaten yolks. Place in a shallow dish. Place a small amount of flour in one hand and shape meat mixture into small balls, about the size of a small egg. Roll each ball in the egg mixture then place in very hot oil. Using a slotted spoon, turn each ball until lightly brown all over. Place on paper towels to drain the excess oils. Makes approximately 4 dozen.

❋ ❋ ❋ ❋ ❋

FRESH FRUIT SALSA

INGREDIENTS:

1 papaya, diced
1 cucumber, diced
1 cup strawberries, cleaned and diced
1 cantaloupe, peeled and diced
3 tablespoons lime juice
3 tablespoons honey

Combine lime juice and honey. In a large bowl, combine fruit. Add honey-lime mixture and chill for 1 hour before serving.

CAMEMBERT QUESADILLA

The full flavor of Camembert cheese makes this
Quesadilla an especially tasty appetizer.

INGREDIENTS:

10 flour tortillas
1 teaspoon butter
1 lb Camembert cheese, cut in strips
2 poblano chiles, roasted, peeled and chopped
1 small onion, sliced thin

Sauté onion slices in butter until tender. Heat flour tortillas by
placing in a large hot pan and heating each side for 10 to
15 seconds. Place Camembert strips, onion slices and chopped
chiles on 1/2 of a flour tortilla and fold. Heat quesadilla until
the cheese melts then cut into triangular wedges. Place in
a warm oven until all tortillas have been filled.

✳ ✳ ✳ ✳ ✳

SOUTHWESTERN SALMON EGGS

INGREDIENTS:

6 hard boiled eggs
2 oz salmon, steamed, boned and flaked
4 tablespoons tomato sauce
1 tablespoon pimento, minced
1/4 tablespoon Worcestershire sauce
1 tablespoon minced fresh onion
2 1/2 tablespoons minced dill pickle
1/4 teaspoon pickle juice
1/8 teaspoon cayenne pepper
2 tablespoons Spanish olives, minced
Salt and pepper

Cut eggs lengthwise, remove yolks. Discard all but 3 of the
egg yolks. In a mixing bowl, combine salmon, tomato
sauce, minced pimento, Worcestershire sauce, minced onion,
minced pickle, pickle juice, cayenne powder, and salt
and pepper to taste. Fill egg whites with mixture and
garnish with minced Spanish olives. Chill to serve.

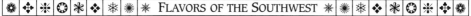

POTATO SKINS

The possibilities for this potato dish are endless.
Fill with cheese and dip in your favorite salsa or
top with shrimp, chives or bacon.

INGREDIENTS:

4 large
baking potatoes
1/4 cup Cheddar
cheese, shredded
Sour Cream
Salt

Clean potatoes well and prick all over with a fork.
Bake potatoes for 45 minutes to 1 hour, until tender
when squeezed. Let cool and then cut in quarters
lengthwise. Preheat oven to 400°F. Cut each in half.
Remove flesh from potato, leaving about 1/8 inch
on the skin. Salt inside skin. Place on baking sheet
and top with cheese. Bake for 12 to 15 minutes,
until skins are crispy and cheese has melted.
Top with a dollop of sour cream.

✳ ✳ ✳ ✳ ✳

CUCUMBER AND MELON SALSA

INGREDIENTS:

1 small cantaloupe
1 papaya
1 cucumber
1/3 cup mint
4 tablespoons lime juice
2 tablespoons honey

Dice cantaloupe, papaya, cucumber and mint, making
sure to remove peel and seeds. Mix lime juice and
honey with fruit and chill before serving.
Makes 4 cups.

✳ ✳ ✳ ✳ ✳

TUNA AND CHILE DIP

An excellent example of the wide variety of foods
to be found in the typical Mexican diet.

INGREDIENTS:

1 7 ounce can tuna, drained
1 tablespoon olive oil
1/2 cup chopped onion
1/4 cup chopped jalapeño peppers
1/4 cup chopped scallions
1/2 cup capers, drained
1/3 cup chopped celery
1 chopped tomato
2 tablespoons lime or lemon juice
1/4 teaspoon seasoned salt
1/2 bag tortilla chips

Combine tuna, olive oil, onion, jalapeño peppers, scallions,
capers, celery, tomato and lemon or lime juice. Salt to taste.
Toss to mix well. Garnish with grated cheese and tortilla chips.

✳ ✳ ✳ ✳ ✳

CAULIFLOWER FRITTERS

INGREDIENTS:

1 pound cauliflower, separated
1 egg
3/4 cup milk
3/4 cup flour
1 teaspoon sugar
3/4 teaspoon baking powder
1/4 teaspoon salt
Dash of nutmeg

Boil separated cauliflower in salted water for 6 to 7 minutes or until
tender. Drain. Heat 1 inch oil in saucepan to 365° F. Beat egg and
milk in a small bowl. Mix sugar, baking powder, flour, salt and nutmeg
in a medium bowl. Stir milk mixture into flour mixture and beat until
smooth. Dip cauliflower into batter. Fry in hot oil until light brown all
over. Place on paper towels to drain excess oil. Serve while hot.

CHILES AND THEIR PREPARATION

Chiles are one of the most important and most often used
ingredients in Southwest cooking. The many varieties
of chiles add a distinctive taste and texture that has
become the trade mark of Southwest cooking.

Preparing fresh chiles is quite easy. Always wear
rubber gloves when handling chiles and make sure your
hands do not come into contact with your eyes, nose or
mouth. The eyes are especially sensitive to chile oils. Wash
chiles and dry well. Char the skin of the chiles over a gas
stove, barbecue, under a broiler, or in a heavy skillet. Turn often
to blacken the skins evenly and to prevent the flesh of the chiles
from burning. When the chiles' skins are black and blistered, place
chiles in a plastic or brown paper bag for 10 minutes. This allows
the steam to loosen the skins from the chiles. Charring the skins
gives the chiles a nice smoky flavor. Wearing rubber gloves,
peel off loosened skin. If you are planning to use the chiles
whole, slit the side of the chile and remove seeds and
stem. Rinse chiles in cold water. Chiles can be
frozen with or without the skin and will
last several months in the freezer.

✳ ✳ ✳ ✳ ✳

FRESH SALSA

This delicious salsa is a wonderful accompaniment
to any Southwestern meal.

INGREDIENTS:

3 large tomatoes, diced
1/2 cup cilantro, chopped
1 medium onion, chopped
4 tablespoons lemon juice
1/4 cup jalapeño
chiles, chopped
Salt and pepper

Mix tomatoes, cilantro, onion, lemon juice, and chiles
together. Salt and pepper to taste. Chill before serving.
Makes 3 cups.

TOMATO AND CHILI SAUCE

This basic tomato based sauce is versatile enough
to be spread over anything from enchiladas
to pasta. The chili powder gives it an
extra boost of flavor.
Make ahead and freeze.

INGREDIENTS:

1/2 cup onion, minced
3 cups tomato purée
1/2 teaspoon garlic powder
3 tablespoons chili powder
2 tablespoons olive oil
1/2 teaspoon basil
1/2 teaspoon oregano
1/8 teaspoon cumin
Salt
Pepper

Saute onion in oil until tender. Add tomato purée,
garlic, chili powder, basil, oregano and cumin.
Stir to mix well and simmer for 1 hour.
Strain mixture. Salt and pepper to taste.
Serve over chicken, enchiladas
or anything tomato sauce is used for.
Makes 4 cups.

A WORD ABOUT FLOUR:

In this book when flour is called for always use
all-purpose flour unless another type
of flour is specified.

✳ ✳ ✳ ✳ ✳

TOMATILLO SAUCE

Tomatillos are an often used vegetable in Mexican cooking. Their bright green color and unique flavor make this sauce very popular throughout the Southwest.

INGREDIENTS:

6 tomatillos
1/2 small onion, chopped
4 serrano chiles, chopped
1 garlic clove, chopped
1/4 teaspoon cumin
2 tablespoons water
2 tablespoons cilantro, chopped
Salt and pepper

Remove the outside skin and stems from tomatillos and rinse in warm water. Simmer for 7 to 10 minutes. Put all ingredients in a food processor and process until the sauce reaches the desired consistency. Add water if necessary. Use extra cilantro leaves for decorative topping.

✳ ✳ ✳ ✳ ✳

GREEN SAUCE

INGREDIENTS:

1 can green chiles, peeled
3/4 cup parsley, chopped
2 1/2 cups chicken broth
2 tablespoons pumpkin seeds
1/4 cup oil
Salt and pepper

Toast pumpkin seeds in oven until lightly brown. Grind pumpkin seeds, using a grinder or blender, add chiles and parsley and grind until fine. Grind two times. Add 1/4 cup chicken broth and strain. Add strained mixture and leftover broth to hot oil and heat. Serve over chicken or fish. Makes almost 1 quart.

CILANTRO SAUCE

This salsa tastes great with shellfish and is also wonderful as a dip or spooned over nachos.

INGREDIENTS:

1 cup fresh cilantro, chopped
1 small onion, chopped
1/2 cup parsley, chopped
1/2 cup olive oil
5 tablespoons lime juice
3 tablespoons distilled white vinegar
1 jalapeno, cleaned and seeded
2 cloves garlic, minced
Salt

Combine cilantro, onion, parsley, oil, lime juice, vinegar, jalapeño, garlic and salt to taste. Mix well and refrigerate for 2 hours. Makes 2 cups.

* * * * *

TACO SAUCE

This versatile salsa can be used as a dip for chips as well as on Tacos and Tostadas.

INGREDIENTS:

2 cups canned tomatoes
1/2 medium onion, diced
1/4 teaspoon garlic powder
1/2 teaspoon oregano
2 canned green chiles, diced
1 dash hot sauce
1 teaspoon salt
1/2 teaspoon pepper

Add onion, chiles, garlic and tomatoes and mash until fine. Add oregano, hot sauce, salt and pepper. Mix well and chill before serving.

Red Chile Salsa

This colorful and versatile sauce can also be used as a
simple salsa served with tortilla chips or over pasta.

INGREDIENTS:

5 dried poblano chiles
1 cup boiling water
1 teaspoon red
chili pepper, crushed
1 cup Italian plum tomatoes,
drained and chopped
1 onion, chopped
1/8 teaspoon garlic powder
1/4 cup olive oil
1 teaspoon sugar
1/2 teaspoon salt
1/4 teaspoon pepper
1 tablespoon lemon juice

Chop poblano chiles, removing stem and seeds.
Place chiles in boiling water and let sit for 1/2 hour.
Drain, and reserve, chile water. Mix chiles, 1/4 cup
chile water, crushed red chili peppers, onion, tomatoes
and garlic powder. Purée mixture in a blender until smooth.
In a small pan, heat olive oil and add purée. Add the
sugar, salt and pepper and cook for 5 minutes.
Remove from heat and let sit for 15 minutes.
Add lemon juice and mix well. Serve warm.
Makes 2 cups.

✳ ✳ ✳ ✳ ✳

A Word About Chiles:

The heat of a chile comes from the capsaicin oil
which is concentrated in the placenta, or veins, of the chile.
The seeds are hot because of their close proximity to
the veins. The **Anaheim** chile, also called **California** chile,
is a large, mild flavored green or yellow chile.

✳ ✳ ✳ ✳ ✳

SOUPS AND SALADS
ALBONDIGAS TO TOMATILLO SALAD

Southwestern soups and salads are as diverse as the Mexican kitchens from which many popular soups originated. Recipes for special soups are often handed down from generation to generation and prized by all family members. The unusual array of ingredients in many of the recipes may seem a trifle odd at first glance, but they are guaranteed to please even the most discerning palate. As the noted Norte Americano food company Campbell Soups has often said, "Soup is good food." The recipes in this chapter are certainly no exception to this rule.

❋ ❋ ❋ ❋ ❋

BLACK BEAN SOUP

This tasty black bean soup is sweeping the Southwest and is found in many of our finest regional cuisine restaurants.

INGREDIENTS:

1 pound dried black beans,
washed thoroughly
2 quarts boiling water
2 tablespoons salt
1/8 teaspoon garlic powder
1 1/2 teaspoons cumin
1 1/2 teaspoons oregano
2 tablespoons white vinegar
10 tablespoons olive oil
1/2 pound onions, chopped
1/2 pound green peppers, chopped

Put beans in large pot and add boiling water. Boil for 2 minutes. Cover and remove from heat. Set aside for 1 hour. Add salt to beans and liquid. Bring to a boil and simmer, covered, for 2 hours, until beans are soft. Put the garlic, cumin, oregano and vinegar into blender and mix into a thick paste. Sauté onion and green pepper in olive oil until tender. Blend in the paste and stir mixture into the beans. Cook over low heat until ready to serve.
Serves 6.

TOMATILLO SALAD

Tomatillos are a small, tomato-like vegetable with
an outer papery husk. Although similar to tomatoes,
they have a unique flavor all their own.

INGREDIENTS:

6 tomatillos
1/4 cup olive oil
2 tablespoons lime juice
1 teaspoon pepper
3/4 cup Parmesan cheese,
grated
1/2 cup piñon nuts

Husk tomatillos and rinse thoroughly. Thinly slice
tomatillos and place on salad plates. Mix olive oil and lime
juice and pepper and pour a small amount over each
plate of sliced tomatillos. Garnish with Parmesan
cheese and piñon nuts.
Serves 4.

✳ ✳ ✳ ✳ ✳

A WORD ABOUT PREPARING BROTHS:

Broths, the base stock of many soups, stews and main
dishes, are extremely important to successful Southwestern
cooking. Chicken broth is made by boiling chicken parts
in 3 or 4 quarts of water. Add onion, garlic and salt and
pepper to taste. Simmer for 1 1/2 hours. Skim off the excess
fat and strain broth. Serve chicken and vegetables and reserve
broth for future use. Beef broth is made by boiling beef bones
in 3 to 6 quarts of water, add onion, salt, pepper and garlic to
taste. Simmer for up to 2 hours. Skim excess fat and strain
broth. Broths can be frozen or refrigerated for later use.

✳ ✳ ✳ ✳ ✳

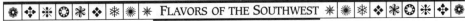
CHILI POBLANO SOUP

This creamy soup is a favorite in kitchens throughout the
Southwest. Serve hot with chile cornbread and a cold cerveza.

INGREDIENTS:

1/4 pound lean pork, cubed
1 small onion, chopped
1 cup corn, fresh from the cob or frozen
1 poblano chile, sliced
1 zucchini, sliced
3 tablespoons tomato purée
1 quart chicken stock
1 avocado, sliced
1/2 cup Monterey Jack cheese,
shredded
Salt and pepper

Brown pork cubes in a medium pan. Add the onion, corn,
poblano chile, zucchini, tomato purée and chicken stock. Add
salt and pepper to taste and simmer for 20 minutes. Garnish
soup with avocado slices and shredded cheese.
Serves 4.

✳ ✳ ✳ ✳ ✳

ORANGE AND ONION SALAD

INGREDIENTS:

2 red onions, cut into rings
1 large orange, cut in chunks
1 can tangerine slices, drained
1 cup sunflower seeds
1 head lettuce, shredded
Cucumber and melon salsa

In a large salad bowl toss onions, orange, tangerine,
sunflower seeds and lettuce. Top with salsa.
Serves 4.

✳ ✳ ✳ ✳ ✳

CHILI CON QUESO SOUP

This thick, rich chili and cheese soup makes a perfect main course when served with warm tortillas or French bread.

INGREDIENTS:

1/2 pound
lean ground beef
1 medium potato,
chopped fine
1 medium onion,
chopped fine
2 green chiles, peeled,
seeded and diced
2 medium tomatoes,
chopped fine
1 1/2 teaspoons chili powder
2 cloves garlic, minced
1 teaspoon oregano
1/2 teaspoon cumin
1 teaspoon salt
1/3 cup flour
4 chicken bouillon cubes
2 quarts hot water
1/3 cup cold water
Tortilla chips
3/4 cup Cheddar cheese,
shredded

In a large pot, cook ground beef, potato, onion, chiles, tomatoes, chili powder, garlic, oregano, cumin and salt. Add bouillon cubes to the hot water and stir until dissolved then add to ground beef mixture. Simmer for 15 minutes. In a separate bowl, mix cold water and flour. Pour slowly into soup, stirring constantly. Simmer for 15 minutes, or until desired thickness is reached. Garnish with tortilla chips and cheese.
Serves 8.

✳ ✳ ✳ ✳ ✳

CHILE AND BEAN SALAD

A cool vegetable salad, just the right thing for
those hot summer nights. Serve with gazpacho
and one of our cool Southwestern desserts.

INGREDIENTS:

1 large bell pepper, seeded
1 16 oz can black beans, drained
1 large tomato, diced
2 jalapeño peppers,
seeded and diced
2 scallions, sliced thin
4 teaspoons lemon juice
3 teaspoons olive oil
Salt and pepper

Combine olive oil, lemon juice, jalapeño peppers and salt and
pepper to taste, set aside. In a salad bowl, combine bell pepper,
black beans, tomato, and scallions. Pour dressing over
all and toss well. Refrigerate before serving.
Serves 4.

❋ ❋ ❋ ❋ ❋

PUMPKIN SOUP

INGREDIENTS:

1 cup canned pumpkin
3 1/2 cups milk
2 tablespoons butter
1/2 teaspoon sugar
1/8 teaspoon nutmeg
1/4 cup sunflower seeds
Pepper
Salt

In a medium sauce pan bring milk to a boil and add pumpkin.
Stir in butter, sugar, nutmeg and salt and pepper. Simmer
over very low heat for 5 to 10 minutes. Garnish with
sunflower seeds.
Serves 4.

TORTILLA SOUP

INGREDIENTS:

2 quarts chicken or beef stock
1/2 cup onion, chopped
1 clove garlic, minced
1 cup tomato sauce
1/2 teaspoon salt
1/4 teaspoon pepper
6 or 8 stale tortillas
1 1/2 cups Monterey Jack
cheese, shredded
Oil for frying

Heat stock, with onion and garlic, to boiling. Simmer for 5 minutes. Add tomato sauce, salt and pepper and simmer for another 5 minutes. Cut tortillas into strips and fry in hot oil until they become crisp. Spoon soup over a handful of tortilla strips to serve. Garnish with grated cheese.

❋ ❋ ❋ ❋ ❋

GREENS WITH CHILES

INGREDIENTS:

1 4 ounce can green
chiles, drained
1 1/2-pounds fresh greens,
spinach,
mustard, or swiss chard
2 tablespoons butter
1/2 cup onion, chopped
1 clove garlic, minced
Salt and pepper

Wash greens well. Cook in a small amount of boiling salted water until tender. Drain and chop. Return to saucepan. Melt butter in a small skillet. Add chiles, onion, and garlic and cook until onion is soft, about 5 minutes. Stir chile mixture into chopped greens. Salt and pepper to taste. Heat thoroughly.
Serves 6.

BELL PEPPER SOUP

INGREDIENTS:

3 red bell peppers,
roasted,
peeled and seeded
1 1/2 cups chicken stock
2 medium carrots,
chopped
1/2 onion, chopped
1/4 cup celery,
chopped
1/3 teaspoon
cayenne pepper
1 cup
whipping cream
Salt

In a saucepan, combine peppers, chicken stock, carrots,
onion, celery and cayenne pepper. Bring to a boil. Simmer over
medium low for 10 minutes. Transfer to a food processor
and purée. Add salt to taste. Return to saucepan and add
cream. Simmer until mixture thickens.

✳ ✳ ✳ ✳ ✳

CHILI AND AVOCADO SOUP

INGREDIENTS:

2 large avocados
2 cups chicken broth
1 1/2 cups half and half
1/4 teaspoon chili powder
Salt
Pepper

Peel and pit avocados and mash. Place mashed avocados
and chicken broth in a medium pan and simmer for 10 minutes,
stirring often. Remove from heat and add half and half, chili
powder and salt and pepper to taste. Stir to mix well
and refrigerate, covered, for 1 hour.
Serves 4.

SOUTHWEST TOMATO SOUP

The jalapeño pepper gives this easy to prepare soup a
special touch and prevents it from being just
another tomato soup recipe.

INGREDIENTS:

3 cups tomato juice
1 6 oz can tomato paste
1 onion, diced
2 slices bacon, chopped
1/8 teaspoon baking soda
1 cup half and half
1 jalapeño pepper, diced
Salt and pepper

In a medium saucepan, cook bacon and onion until onion
becomes tender. Add tomato juice, tomato paste, baking
soda and salt and pepper to taste. Simmer over very low heat
for 10 minutes then add half and half. Stir and cook until soup
just becomes hot, do not bring soup to a boil.
Garnish with diced jalapeño pepper.
Serves 6.

✳ ✳ ✳ ✳ ✳

GARLIC CROUTONS

INGREDIENTS:

1 loaf stale bread
1/2 cup butter
1/4 cup olive oil
3/4 teaspoon garlic powder
2 tablespoons parsley
Salt
Pepper

Cut bread into 1 inch cubes and spread evenly over baking sheet.
Let dry completely. In a large skillet, heat butter and oil and
add garlic, parsley, and salt and pepper to taste. Place cubes
into a large bowl and pour butter mixture over croutons.
Fry to a light brown.

ZUCCHINI SOUP

This distinctive soup can be served hot or cold and
is a wonderful starter for chicken or fish dinners.

INGREDIENTS:

4 large zucchini
2 cups water
1 cup chicken broth
2 tablespoons parsley leaves
2 tablespoons butter
1 13 ounce can evaporated milk
1 tablespoon onion, diced
1 tablespoon flour
Parsley
Salt and pepper

Cut zucchini into large pieces, make sure to wash and cut
stems first. Place zucchini and water in a pot and bring
to a boil. Cover pot and simmer for 15 minutes. Remove
from heat and let cool. Strain zucchini, reserving
1 cup cooking liquid, and place in a blender.
Add 2 tablespoons parsley and 1 cup of the cooking
liquid and purée. Sauté onion in butter until tender. Add flour
and cook for 1 minute, stirring. Add puréed zucchini,
evaporated milk, chicken broth and salt. Cook over medium
heat, stirring often, until soup comes to a boil.
Garnish with parsley leaves.
Serves 6.

✳ ✳ ✳ ✳ ✳

A WORD ABOUT ARTICHOKES:

When buying fresh artichokes, look for a solid head of about
3 to 3 1/2 inches in diameter. Avoid the larger artichokes because
they tend to be too fibrous. Check the outside and avoid
artichokes with brown, cracked or withered stems or leaves,
this shows age. Fresh artichokes, stored in a closed bags in
the refrigerator, will last 2 to 3 days.

✳ ✳ ✳ ✳ ✳

PRICKLY PEAR SALAD

Picking the fruit from a prickly pear cactus can be quite a challenge, but it is certainly worth the effort! Choose either the yellow spine prickly or the desert prickly pear cactus for the best tasting prickly pear fruit.

INGREDIENTS:

1/4 cup orange juice
1/3 cup 7-Up
1 teaspoon ginger root, grated
1 tablespoon lemon juice
2 tablespoons sugar
1 peach, peeled and sliced
1 pear, peeled and sliced
1 cup strawberries, sliced
1/4 cup prickly pear
fruit, diced
Mixed salad greens

To prepare prickly pear fruit, place in boiling water for 1 minute, then dip in cold water. Use a knife to slice and peel skin, scraping off any needles. Dice and add to other diced fruit. Combine orange juice, 7-Up, ginger root, lemon juice and sugar. Mix well and pour over fruit. Chill before serving on a bed of salad greens.

✳ ✳ ✳ ✳ ✳

PRICKLY PEAR VINAIGRETTE

INGREDIENTS:

4 prickly pear fruits,
cleaned and puréed
6 ounces olive oil
2 ounces cider vinegar
2 tablespoons onion, chopped
1 teaspoon Dijon mustard

Combine purée with olive oil, cider vinegar, onion and Dijon mustard. Mix well and store covered. Makes 1 1/2 cups.

✳ ✳ ✳ ✳ ✳

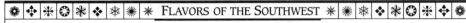
CUCUMBER SALAD

This cool, zesty salad is an excellent side dish
and goes well with grilled meats. For extra color,
garnish with mandarin orange slices.

INGREDIENTS:

3 large cucumbers
1/3 cup vinegar
2 tablespoons water
1/4 cup sugar
1 teaspoon salt
1/4 teaspoon ground pepper
1 tablespoon minced dill

Peel cucumbers and slice very thin. Refrigerate slices in a bowl
of ice water for at least 1 hour. In a small mixing bowl, combine
vinegar, water, sugar, and salt and pepper. Drain cucumbers
and pat dry. Place slices in a bowl and pour vinegar mixture
over top. Refrigerate for 1 hour. Garnish with dill before serving.
Serves 6.

TRIPE SOUP

INGREDIENTS:

2 calves' feet
5 lbs tripe, fresh or pickled
3 cups canned hominy
4 quarts water
2 medium onions, minced
4 cloves garlic, minced
1 1/2 tablespoons salt
1 tablespoon oregano

Cool calves' feet in 4 quarts of cold water for 1 1/2 hours and
cut into small pieces. Wash tripe and cut into small pieces
and add to calves' feet. Add onion, garlic, oregano and salt.
Simmer on low heat for 4 hours. Add hominy
and simmer for 2 1/2 hours.
Serves 16.

CHRISTMAS EVE SALAD

This fruit salad is a traditional Mexican Christmas salad.

INGREDIENTS:

1/4 cup white vinegar
3 tablespoons orange juice
1 tablespoon lime juice
1 teaspoon salt
1 teaspoon sugar
1 clove garlic
1/4 teaspoon paprika
1/8 teaspoon white pepper
2/3 cup vegetable oil
3/4 cup pine nuts
3 oranges, peeled
3 limes, sliced thin and quartered
3 carrots, peeled, cut into 1/4x2 inch
julienne, blanched 1 minute and chilled
2 ripe bananas, halved lengthwise,
sliced and sprinkled with lime juice
1 jicama, peeled and cut in
1/4x2 inch julienne
5 large beets, cooked, chilled and
cut into 1/4x2 inch julienne
1 romaine lettuce head, cut
crosswise into 2 inch thick slices
1/2 fresh pineapple, cut in
1/4x2 inch strips

To prepare dressing, mince garlic in processor. Blend in vinegar, orange and lime juice, salt sugar, paprika and pepper. Keep machine running, add oil in steady stream and mix until creamy. Heat 2 tablespoons dressing in medium skillet on medium-high heat. Add nuts and sauté until golden. Drain nuts on paper towels to absorb excess oil. Combine oranges, limes, carrots, bananas and jicama in large bowl. Pour 2/3 of the dressing over top and toss gently to coat. Add remaining dressing to the beets and toss. To arrange, line platter with lettuce slices. Arrange beets pinwheel style in center of platter. Mound fruit and vegetables around beets to create a lovely salad. Garnish with pineapple slices.
Serves 6.

CORN SOUP

Corn soup was first prepared by Southwestern
Native Americans before the birth of Christ.

INGREDIENTS:

4 cups fresh corn
1 cup chicken stock
1/4 cup butter
4 cups milk
1/2 cup
green onion, chopped
6 tablespoons sour cream
3 tablespoons
green chiles, diced
Salt and pepper

Blend corn and chicken stock to a smooth purée.
Sauté green onions in butter until tender. Add purée
and cook over medium heat for about 8 minutes, or until
thickened. Add milk and salt and pepper to taste and
cook for 10 minutes. Garnish with sour cream and chiles.

✳ ✳ ✳ ✳ ✳

CLAM SOUP

INGREDIENTS:

2 cans clams, with juice
1 medium onion, diced
1 clove garlic
4 tablespoons olive oil
1/2 cup tomato sauce
1 sprig parsley, minced
Salt and pepper

Sauté onion in oil and add parsley, tomato sauce and
garlic. Add clams with juice and salt and pepper
to taste. Heat thoroughly.
Serves 4.

✳ ✳ ✳ ✳ ✳

ALBONDIGAS

Perhaps the most famous of all Mexican soups, this
meatball soup is found all over the Southwest.

INGREDIENTS:

1 medium onion,
minced
1/4 teaspoon
garlic powder
1/2 can
tomato sauce
2 tablespoons oil
3 quarts beef stock
3/4 pound ground beef
3/4 pound ground pork
1/3 cup
uncooked rice
2 teaspoons salt
1/2 teaspoon pepper
1 egg, beaten
Sprig of mint, diced

Sauté onion in oil, add garlic powder and mix gently.
Add tomato sauce and beef stock. Bring to a boil.
Mix meat with egg, rice, mint, salt and pepper and shape
into small balls. Add balls to boiling broth, cover tightly.
Cook for 30 minutes.
Serves 8.

❋　❋　❋　❋　❋

A WORD ABOUT SEASONINGS:

For additional flavor in Mexican and
Southwestern soups add hot salsa or lime
juice after serving to individual
taste. Remember, a little
hot salsa can go a long way.

❋　❋　❋　❋　❋

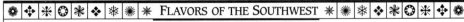

ASPARAGUS AND BLACK BEAN SALAD

A colorful and very tasty cold salad that is an excellent addition to any barbeque. The cilantro dressing gives it a wonderfully fresh and zesty flavor.

INGREDIENTS FOR SALAD:

1 pound fresh asparagus
1 16 oz can black beans,
drained
2 tablespoons
chopped onion
1 tomato, chopped

INGREDIENTS FOR DRESSING:

3 tablespoons olive oil
2 tablespoons red
wine vinegar
1 clove garlic, crushed
1 tablespoon cilantro,
chopped
1/2 teaspoon
ground cumin
Salt
Pepper

Break off ends of asparagus and wash, removing scales if tough. Cut into 1 inch pieces. Place steamer basket in less than 1/2 inch water, making sure the water does not touch the asparagus. Cover and bring to a boil. Reduce heat and steam for 6 minutes. When asparagus has cooled, add black beans, tomato, and onion. Refrigerate for several hours In a separate bowl, combine olive oil, red wine vinegar, garlic, cilantro, cumin and salt and pepper to taste. Shake well before pouring over asparagus and black beans.
Serve on a bed of lettuce
Serves 6.

✳ ✳ ✳ ✳ ✳

DESERT ORIENTAL SALAD

A touch of the Orient with a Southwestern flavor. This makes a refreshingly light meal for a hot summer night.

INGREDIENTS FOR SALAD:

2 tablespoons sugar
1/2 cup
sliced almonds
1/2 head iceberg lettuce
1/2 head
romaine lettuce
1 cup chopped celery
2 green onions,
chopped
1 11 oz can mandarin
oranges, drained
1 avocado,
sliced

INGREDIENTS FOR DRESSING:

2 tablespoons
orange juice
1/4 teaspoon grated
orange peel
1/4 teaspoon salt
1/4 cup oil
1 tablespoon red
wine vinegar
1 tablespoon sugar

For the dressing; combine orange juice, grated peel, salt, oil, vinegar and sugar and mix well. In a small pan, heat sugar and almonds until sugar is dissolved and almonds are coated. Shred and mix lettuce, celery and onions, avocado and mandarin oranges. Pour dressing over all and top with almonds.

✳ ✳ ✳ ✳ ✳

SEDONA SQUASH SOUP

The deep orange color of the squash gives this soup colors reminiscent of the natural beauty of Sedona, Arizona.

INGREDIENTS:

2 large onions,
chopped
1/4 cup oil
4 1/2 cups vegetable broth
1/2 cup lentils
1 1/2 cups puréed squash
1 teaspoon marjoram
1 teaspoon thyme
1/4 teaspoon pepper
Salt

Sauté onions in oil until tender. Add vegetable broth, lentils and squash, simmer for 30 minutes. Add marjoram, thyme, pepper and salt to taste. Simmer for 45 minutes.
Serves 6.

✳ ✳ ✳ ✳ ✳

SOUTHWESTERN COLESLAW

INGREDIENTS:

1 head green cabbage
2 carrots
1 onion
1/2 red bell pepper
5 tablespoons mayonnaise
1 tablespoon Dijon mustard
3 tablespoons cider vinegar
2 teaspoons sugar
1 tablespoon salt

Shred cabbage and grate the carrots, bell pepper, and onion. Combine mayonnaise, Dijon mustard, cider vinegar, sugar and salt and mix well. Pour over grated vegetables and toss well. Refrigerate before serving.

✳ ✳ ✳ ✳ ✳

BEER AND CHEESE SOUP

A Mexican favorite with a little something extra.
Always popular while watching bull
fights and soccer games.

INGREDIENTS:

1/2 cup chopped onion
2 tablespoons butter
1 bottle of Mexican beer
1/2 cup celery, diced
1/2 cup carrots, diced
2 cups chicken broth
1 teaspoon salt
1 cup sour cream
1 1/2 cups Monterey
Jack cheese
1/4 teaspoon nutmeg
Salt to taste
Pepper to taste

Sauté onion in butter until tender. Add beer and
vegetables, stir gently. Bring to a boil and reduce heat before
covering. Let simmer for 7 to 10 minutes. Add chicken
broth, nutmeg, salt and pepper. Bring to a boil and reduce
heat. Simmer for 30 minutes, covered. Stir in sour cream when
pot is removed from heat and garnish with cheese.
Serves 6.

✳ ✳ ✳ ✳ ✳

A WORD ABOUT SALADS:

For a quick and easy salad that has a beautiful
appearance, peel a ripe tomato
or a bell pepper and fill with
Guacamole or a cucumber
and melon salsa.

✳ ✳ ✳ ✳ ✳

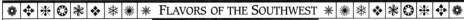
RICH RICE
AND NUT SALAD

You will love this wonderfully flavored rice salad.
Serve with a loaf of crusty french bread
and a glass of wine.

INGREDIENTS:

1 1/2 cups cooked
brown rice
2 tablespoons
olive oil
2 tablespoons
lemon juice
1/4 cucumber,
chopped
5 black olives,
pitted and chopped
1/2 cup cashews,
chopped
1/2 cup walnuts,
chopped
1/2 cup blanched almonds,
chopped
1/2 cup golden raisins
1/4 cup currants
1 15 oz can peach slices
Salt
Pepper

Combine olive oil, lemon juice and salt and pepper to
taste. Mix well and set aside. Soak dried fruits until
thoroughly moist, drain. In a large bowl, combine
cooked rice, cucumber, black olives, nuts, softened
fruit, and peaches. Shake dressing well and pour
over salad, toss well. Serve on a bed of lettuce.
Serves 4.

✳ ✳ ✳ ✳ ✳

SPINACH SALAD

A basic and healthy salad that can be
adapted to your own tastes.

INGREDIENTS FOR SALAD:

2 bunches of spinach,
trimmed and cleaned
2 bunches
watercress

INGREDIENTS FOR
POPPY SEED DRESSING:

1/2 cup sugar
1 teaspoon salt
1 teaspoon
dry mustard
1/2 teaspoon
onion powder
1/3 cup white
balsamic vinegar
1 cup oil
1 tablespoon
lime juice
1 1/2 tablespoons
poppy seed

Mix sugar, salt, mustard, onion powder,
white balsamic vinegar, and lime juice.
Stir to dissolve sugar.
Stir in oil slowly, beating well.
Add poppy seeds. Chill before
pouring over mixed greens.
Serves 4.

✳ ✳ ✳ ✳ ✳

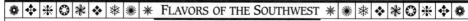

SALSA AND AVOCADO SALAD

Featuring avocados and bell peppers, favorite foods of the Southwest, this salad combines smooth and creamy texture of avocados with the crisp bite of tangy salad greens.

INGREDIENTS FOR SALAD:

1/4 pound romaine lettuce
1/4 pound radicchio
1/4 pound arugula
1 Belgian endive
4 ozs radish sprouts
4 ounces goat cheese,
sliced
2 avocados

INGREDIENTS FOR SALSA:

1 red bell pepper,
diced
1 orange bell pepper,
diced
1 yellow bell pepper,
diced
1 green onion,
chopped
1 medium tomato,
chopped
1 tablespoon cilantro,
chopped
1 tablespoon olive oil
Juice from 1 lemon
Salt and pepper

Peel and cut avocados in half, removing pit. In a small bowl, mix red, orange and yellow bell peppers, onion, tomato, cilantro, olive oil, lemon juice and salt and pepper to taste. Wash salad greens and arrange on 4 plates. Fill avocados half way with salsa. and cover with slice of goat cheese. Broil for 2 minutes and place on lettuce to serve.
Serves 4.

❋ ❋ ❋ ❋ ❋

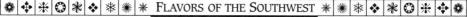
COLD APPLE SOUP

A cool and refreshing dish to serve as a light meal,
and an excellent starter to grilled meats.

INGREDIENTS:

4 1/2 Granny
Smith apples
1 cup dry
white wine
2 cinnamon sticks
2 slices fresh ginger
5 tablespoons sugar
1 tablespoon apple
brandy
1/4 cup sour cream
1 cup beef stock
1 cup heavy cream
1/2 teaspoon salt
Juice from 1 lemon

Peel, core and cut 4 apples into quarters. Take the
half apple and dice well. Sprinkle diced apple with lemon
juice and set aside. In a large saucepan, combine
quartered apples, wine, cinnamon sticks, ginger and sugar.
Bring to a boil before covering and reduce heat. Cook over
medium heat for 10 minutes. Cool and discard cinnamon
sticks and ginger. Place remaining mixture, apples
included, into a blender with the apple brandy and
sour cream. Blend until smooth then add stock and
cream, while the blender is running. Add remaining
lemon juice and salt, again while the blender is
still running. Chill, and garnish with diced
apples before serving.
Serves 4.

✳ ✳ ✳ ✳ ✳

A WORD ABOUT SPICES:

Paprika, made from dried red bell peppers,
is high in vitamins A and C.

✳ ✳ ✳ ✳ ✳

TOSSED GREEN SALAD

The chili powder and other seasonings give
this green salad a real spark of flavor.

INGREDIENTS:

1 cup mushrooms, sliced
1 cup cauliflower, separated
1 cup zucchini, sliced
1 small turnip, grated
1/2 cucumber, sliced
1/2 onion, sliced
1/2 piece of celery, chopped
10 olives, sliced
1/4 cup Cheddar cheese, shredded
1/4 cup Monterey Jack Cheese,
shredded
1/2 cup sour cream
4 hard boiled eggs, sliced
1 teaspoon cider vinegar
1/2 cup mayonnaise
1/2 teaspoon chili powder
1/2 teaspoon salt
1/2 teaspoon pepper
1/2 teaspoon garlic powder
1/2 teaspoon celery seed
1/2 teaspoon paprika
1/2 teaspoon cilantro
1/2 teaspoon red hot chili seeds
2 tablespoons sunflower seeds

In a very large salad bowl, combine mushrooms,
cauliflower, zucchini, shredded turnip, cucumber, onion,
celery, olives, and hard boiled eggs. Place bowl in the
refrigerator until ready to serve. In a small mixing bowl,
blend sour cream, cider vinegar, mayonnaise, chili powder,
salt, pepper, garlic powder, celery seed, paprika, cilantro,
red hot chili seeds and mix well. When ready to serve salad,
pour dressing over the top and garnish with shredded cheese
and sunflower seeds, or serve dressing on the side.

✻ ✻ ✻ ✻ ✻

MEXICAN CHEF'S SALAD

This recipe combines common ingredients used in many
Mexican dishes; beans, tortillas, chiles, cheeses and fresh
vegetables. What a combination!

INGREDIENTS:

2 corn tortillas, fried crisp
1/2 cup refried beans, heated
1 cup sliced turkey
1 medium avocado, peeled,
pitted and sliced lengthwise
1/3 cup Cheddar cheese,
shredded
1 can green chiles,
seeded and chopped
1/4 cup Romano cheese,
grated
2 medium tomatoes,
cut in wedges
1 teaspoon jalapeño chile,
minced
1/2 cup green onion, chopped
2 cups cooked peas, cold
5 cups shredded lettuce
2 tablespoons lemon juice
1/4 cup oil
Salt
Pepper

To make the lettuce layer, mix peas with jalapeño
chile, green onion, oil, lettuce, vinegar and salt and pepper
to taste. Spread beans over tortillas. Place bean-coated
tortillas on separate plates and place a mound of chef's
lettuce layer in the center of each tortilla. Place strips of
turkey around sides of lettuce. Fill in empty spaces
with slices of avocado and spread shredded
cheese and chiles over top. Garnish with Romano
cheese and tomato wedges.
Serves 2.

✳ ✳ ✳ ✳ ✳

WARM SCALLOP SALAD

This dish is a perfect example of the uniqueness
and diversity of the Mexican diet.

INGREDIENTS:

2 cups chicken broth
1/3 pound fresh sea scallops
1/4 cup olive oil
1 1/2 tablespoons Dijon mustard
8 large spinach leaves, stemmed
1 medium avocado, peeled,
pitted and thinly sliced
Salt and pepper to taste

Heat broth to low simmer in medium saucepan. Add scallops
and poach until opaque, about 2 to 3 minutes. Do not over
cook or scallops will be tough. Chill scallops in broth by
setting pan in bowl of ice water for about 30 minutes. Slice
cooled scallops thin. Combine oil, vinegar, mustard, salt and
pepper in a small saucepan and simmer gently. Stack
spinach leaves and roll up lengthwise. Cut crosswise. Divide
spinach between 2 heated plates. Arrange scallops and
avocado decoratively on spinach. Pour warm dressing
over salads and serve immediately. Serves 2.

✳ ✳ ✳ ✳ ✳

PAPAYA AND AVOCADO SALAD

INGREDIENTS:

1 head of lettuce
1 ripe papaya, peeled and sliced
2 ripe avocados, peeled and sliced
1/4 cup lime juice
1/4 cup olive oil
Salt and pepper to taste

Divide lettuce and place on six plates. Place papaya
and avocado slices in alternating layers over lettuce. Combine
lime juice, olive oil and salt and pepper to taste and pour
over papaya and avocado layers. Serves 6.

SWEET POTATO SOUP

This creamy creation is an excellent starter dish.

INGREDIENTS:

4 large sweet potatoes,
peeled
Chicken stock
2 green leeks, chopped
2 tablespoons butter
1 cup whipping cream
1/2 teaspoon white pepper
2 tablespoons chives,
chopped
1 teaspoon thyme

Cut sweet potatoes into large pieces and place in a medium pot. Add chicken stock to cover. Melt butter and sauté leeks. Add to pot with sweet potatoes. Cook potatoes over medium heat until done. Set aside to cool. Transfer sweet potatoes to blender or food processor and purée to smooth consistency. Add cream to desired consistency. Add pepper and thyme to taste. Chill and garnish with chives before serving.

✳ ✳ ✳ ✳ ✳

AVOCADO SOUP

INGREDIENTS:

2 ripe avocados, cut in slices
3 small onions, chopped
1/2 cup light cream
1/2 cup heavy cream
3/4 cup water
1 teaspoon salt
1 teaspoon pepper

Place avocados, onions and heavy cream in a blender. Blend until reaching a thick, smooth consistency. Add light cream, water, salt and pepper and puree until smooth. Add water to achieve a thinner consistency, if desired.

GAZPACHO

This cold tomato soup is a traditional Mexican dish,
just perfect for those hot days of summer.

INGREDIENTS:

10 ounces tomato juice
2 medium tomatoes,
chopped
1 tablespoon sugar
1/4 teaspoon salt
1/4 cup red wine vinegar
1/4 cup salad oil
1 small onion,
finely chopped
2 celery stalks, diced
2 green onions,
chopped
1/2 medium cucumber,
chopped
1 small green pepper,
finely chopped

Blend together tomato juice, 1/2 of chopped tomatoes,
sugar, salt, vinegar and oil in a blender. Add remaining
tomatoes, onion, celery, cucumber and green pepper
and mix well. Serve cold, add sour cream, croutons
and shredded cheese to taste.
Serves 6.

❋ ❋ ❋ ❋ ❋

A WORD ABOUT CHILES:

Jalapeño chiles are small green chiles with a fiery flavor.
Chipotle chiles are smoked and dried Jalapeno's that have
a smoky flavor that is very hot. California chiles, also called
Anaheim chiles, are large green chiles with a mild flavor
Not all chiles of the same type possess the same flavor.
Sample before using to determine degree of heat.

❋ ❋ ❋ ❋ ❋

TORTILLAS AND BREADS
BLUE CORN TORTILLAS TO ZUCCHINI BREAD

Tortillas are a versatile food with many uses in the
Southwestern kitchen and are an important ingredient in
dishes such as Enchiladas, Tacos and Fajitas. Tortillas are made
from both corn and flour with corn tortillas the most common
tortilla made in Mexico. Flour tortillas are more popular in
Southwestern cooking. Corn breads are almost as popular
in the Southwest as tortillas but are not as versatile.
Tortillas as can be fried for crisp shells, steamed to
create soft tacos. In the Mexican kitchen tortillas
never go to waste. Use stale tortillas in
casserole dishes or fry them to make
chips for salsas and dips.

FLOUR TORTILLAS

Flour tortillas were introduced to Mexico by the Spanish
who brought wheat to the new country. They are most
popular in Northern Mexico and the Southwestern
part of the United States.

INGREDIENTS:

2 cups flour
1/4 cup lard
3/4 cup warm water
1/2 teaspoon salt

Combine flour and salt in a large mixing bowl. Add lard,
using fingers, until well mixed. Add water, a little at a time,
until dough forms a shiny ball. Pinch off balls of dough
and roll out onto a floured board or pastry cloth to
desired size. Cook on a preheated griddle or comal for
1 to 2 minutes, until bubbles appear on top. Turn tortillas
over and cook the other side. Serve warm.
Makes 12 tortillas.

CORN TORTILLAS

Corn tortillas are the most popular tortilla in Mexico.
Although the quality of store-bought tortillas is acceptable,
nothing beats the freshness of home-made tortillas.

INGREDIENTS:

2 cups masa harina
1 1/2 cups warm water

Mix masa harina with 1 cup warm water.
Add more water if needed to make dough hold.
Shape dough into a ball and divide into 12 pieces.
Roll pieces into balls. Place a flattened ball of dough
between layers of dampened cheese cloth. Roll with
light strokes until dough is about 6 inches around. Pull
back cloth carefully and trim to make round. Place tortilla
on a sheet of waxed paper and layer paper between each
tortilla. To cook, peel off top layer of waxed paper. Place
tortilla, paper side up, on an ungreased griddle or frying
pan, preheated to medium. Peel off remaining paper as
tortilla warms. Cook 1 to 2 minutes, turn often. Tortilla
is done when it looks dry and is flecked with light
brown spots. Can be reheated. Makes 12 tortillas.

TO REHEAT TORTILLAS:

To soften a single tortilla, place tortilla on an
ungreased warm griddle or frying pan.
Turn often until soft, about 30 seconds. To
reheat a package of tortillas in a microwave oven,
poke holes in package and
microwave for 1 minute.

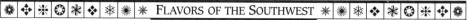

ZUCCHINI BREAD

This bread is so versatile! You can prepare it in a hurry and freeze it for future use. A loaf of Zucchini Bread also makes a lovely home-made gift during the holidays season.

INGREDIENTS:

3 eggs
2 cups
granulated sugar
2 cups
grated zucchini,
packed tight
1 cup oil
1 teaspoon vanilla
3 cups flour
1 teaspoon
baking soda
1 teaspoon
baking powder
1/2 teaspoon salt
1 teaspoon ginger
1 teaspoon cinnamon
1/2 teaspoon
ground cloves
1 cup walnuts,
chopped

Preheat oven to 325°F. Combine eggs, sugar and oil. Add zucchini and vanilla, mix well. Sift together, flour, baking soda, baking powder, salt, ginger, cinnamon and cloves. Add to egg mixture slowly, using a mixer until blended well. Add walnuts and pour into greased 5x8 inch loaf pans. Bake for 1 hour. Cool for 1/2 hour before removing from pans.

MEXICAN CORN BREAD

Mild green chiles give this colorful corn bread its unique
flavor. Serve with chile butter for an extra zing.

INGREDIENTS:

1 1/2 cups cornmeal
2 tablespoons bacon drippings
1 1/2 tablespoons flour
1 tablespoon salt
1/2 teaspoon baking soda
1 cup buttermilk
2/3 cup oil
2 eggs, beaten
1 8 ounce can cream corn
1 4 ounce can green chiles,
drained and chopped
4 green onions, chopped
1 1/2 cups Monterey Jack cheese,
shredded

Mix cornmeal, flour, salt and baking soda in a mixing
bowl. Add buttermilk, oil, eggs and corn and mix well.
Stir in chiles and onions. Preheat oven to 375°F.
Grease a large baking dish with bacon fat, heat in oven.
Pour half the batter into heated pan and sprinkle with
half the cheese. Repeat process using remaining batter
and cheese. Bake for 35 minutes. Cut and serve warm.
Serves 8.

TORTILLA CHIPS

INGREDIENTS:

8 corn tortillas
Salt
Oil

Cut tortillas in half then down to eighths. Heat oil to
about 350°F and fry until crisp. Place on paper
towels to drain excess oil. Salt to taste.
Makes 32.

CORNBREAD PIE

This cornbread is easy to prepare and is very tasty.
Serve with your hottest bowl of chili.

INGREDIENTS:

1 cup
butter, softened
1 cup sugar
1 17 ounce
can cream corn
1 cup Monterey
Jack cheese, shredded
4 eggs
1 4 ounce can
green chiles, drained,
seeded, and chopped
1 cup yellow cornmeal
1 cup flour
4 teaspoons
baking powder
1/2 teaspoon salt

Cream butter and sugar until light and fluffy.
Beat in eggs, one at a time. Stir in corn, cheese,
chiles and cornmeal. Sift flour, baking powder and
salt and stir into batter. Preheat oven to 300°F.
Pour mixture into greased 13x9 inch baking pan and
bake for 1 hour, until a wooden pick inserted in
center comes out clean. Serve hot.
Serves 8.

A WORD ABOUT TORTILLA UTENSILS:

A **comal** is a griddle used for baking or heating tortillas.
Bolillos are short rolling pins that are two inches in
diameter and are used to roll flour tortillas to the correct
thickness. They are also used to roll corn tortillas, however,
a **tortilla press** works best when making corn tortillas.

CHOCOLATE CHIP AND ORANGE MUFFINS

Muffins are an excellent choice for a light breakfast or treat and these Chocolate Chip and Orange Muffins are especially tasty.

INGREDIENTS:

1/2 cup oil
1 egg, beaten
3/4 cup milk
1 teaspoon vanilla
2 cups flour
1 cup sugar
1 teaspoon salt
1 tablespoon baking powder
1 cup mini semisweet chocolate chips
2 tablespoons orange peel, freshly grated

Mix oil, beaten egg, milk and vanilla in a medium mixing bowl. Combine flour, sugar, salt and baking powder. Add to egg and milk mixture and gently mix. Preheat oven to 400°F. Grease a muffin tray. Fold orange peel and chocolate chips into batter before pouring batter into the muffin cups. Bake for 20 minutes. Makes 12 muffins.

CHILI BUTTER

INGREDIENTS:

1/2 pound butter
1 teaspoon chili powder
1 teaspoon garlic powder
2 tablespoons lemon juice

When butter is room temperature, add salt, chili powder, garlic powder and lemon juice. Mix well and chill. Refrigerate after using.

BLUE CORN BREAD WITH CHILES

Corn bread is a wonderful comfort food, and this is a special recipe. As well as tasting lovely, its appearance on the plate is quite attractive.

INGREDIENTS:

1 1/2 cups
blue cornmeal
1/2 cup flour
1/2 teaspoon salt
1 Tbsp baking powder
1/4 cup onion,
chopped fine
1/2 cup butter, melted
3 jalapeño
peppers, chopped
1 1/2 cups
Monterey Jack
cheese, shredded
1 cup milk

Preheat oven to 350°F. Combine flour, cornmeal, baking powder, onions and salt. Add milk and butter and mix thoroughly. In a separate bowl, combine cheese and jalapeños. Grease a medium sized baking pan and pour 1/2 of the batter into pan. Spread the cheese and jalapeño mixture evenly over batter. Pour remaining batter over cheese and cook for 1 hour. Let cool and cut into squares.
Serves 8.

A WORD ABOUT FLOUR:

When baking, always use **all-purpose** flour unless otherwise specified.

MEXICAN HARD ROLLS

These hard rolls are just the perfect thing
to serve with stews, soups and salads.
To store, wrap tightly in plastic.

INGREDIENTS:

6 cups flour
1 package yeast
2 teaspoons sugar
1 teaspoon salt
1 3/4 cups
warm water

In a large bowl, combine yeast and sugar then add warm
water. Add salt and flour, one cup at a time beating well.
Knead dough on a floured surface for about 10 minutes,
until dough becomes smooth. Place dough in a greased bowl
and cover with waxed paper. Place bowl in a warm place
and let rise. When dough doubles its size punch down and let
rise again, until doubled again. Cut dough into 35 pieces of
equal size and shape into long thin rolls. Twist the ends and place
on a floured baking sheet. Cut a slash in the tops of the rolls
with a sharp knife and cover with a towel . Let dough rise until
doubled in size. Preheat oven to 400°F. When rolls have almost
doubled, brush tops with melted butter and bake for 20 to 30
minutes, or until tops become light brown.

HONEY BUTTER

INGREDIENTS:

1/2 pound butter
1/4 cup honey

When butter is room temperature, add honey.
Mix well and chill. Refrigerate after using.

BUTTERMILK BISCUITS

These biscuits may have originated in the deep south, but they have been cherished by Southwesterners, especially cowboys, for generations.

INGREDIENTS

1/3 cup shortening
1 3/4 cups flour
2 teaspoons
baking powder
1/4 teaspoon
baking soda
3/4 teaspoon salt
3/4 cup buttermilk

Preheat oven to 450°F. Using two knives or a pastry blender, cut shortening into flour, baking powder, baking soda and salt until mixture turns into fine crumbs. Add buttermilk, a little at a time, until dough leaves side of bowl and becomes a ball. Turn dough onto a floured surface. Knead lightly, about 10 times. Roll out dough to 1/4 inch thick. Cut with a floured biscuit cutter. On an ungreased cookie sheet, place biscuits about 1 inch apart. Bake for 10 to 12 minutes, until light brown. Remove from cookie sheet immediately to cool. Serve with honey butter or jam. Makes 1 dozen.

A WORD ABOUT BISCUIT VARIATIONS:

Add 1/2 cup shredded Cheddar cheese to make **Cheese Biscuits**. For **Cornmeal Biscuits** substitute 1/2 cup cornmeal for 1/2 cup flour. Sprinkle cookie sheet with cornmeal and then sprinkle cornmeal over biscuits before cooking.

SOPAIPILLAS

A type of Mexican doughnut, Sopaipillas
are often sold at carnivals and fairs all
over the Southwest as well as by
street vendors in Mexico.

INGREDIENTS:

2 cups flour
2 teaspoons
baking powder
1 tablespoon shortening
1/2 teaspoon salt
3/4 cup warm water
Oil for frying
Honey

Mix flour, salt and baking powder in medium
mixing bowl. Cut in shortening until evenly
blended. Add warm water until all ingredients are
moist. Place dough on a lightly floured surface.
Knead for about 5 minutes until smooth.
Wrap dough in plastic wrap and let sit
for 30 minutes. Separate dough in
half and roll each ball on a lightly floured
board. Roll out each ball into a circle about
1/8 inches thick. Cut into 8 pie-shaped
pieces. Heat 1 1/2 inches of oil in a
skillet to 400°F. Gently place
wedges of dough in hot oil. Cook until
puffy and golden brown, turning once.
If wedges do not puff up right away,
the oil is not hot enough. Place
cooked sopaipillas on paper
towel to drain excess oil.
Serve warm with honey.
Makes 16.

POLENTA CAKES

These corn cakes are an excellent
accompaniment to beef and chicken, as well
as most pasta dishes.

INGREDIENTS:

1 quart water
1 teaspoon salt
1 cup yellow cornmeal,
coarsely ground
1 teaspoon paprika
1/4 teaspoon
cayenne pepper
2 tablespoons Parmesan
cheese, grated
1/4 cup butter

Boil salted water and gradually stir in corn meal.
Cook over low heat, stirring often, for 15 minutes
or until mixture pulls away from the sides of pan.
Beat in paprika, cayenne pepper and grated Parmesan
cheese. Spread mixture in a greased pan to form a
layer 1/2 inch thick. Chill until set. Cut into squares
and sauté in butter until brown on both sides.
Makes from 10 to 12 squares.

A WORD ABOUT CORN:

The history of the Southwest reflects the ancient Indians
belief that man was created from corn by the gods.
Today, corn is still considered an important
crop and is the main ingredient in
many recipes, from basic meals to
desserts and beverages.

CHILI AND STEWS
LONGSTANDING TEXAS TRADITIONS

Chili, commonly believed to have originated in San Antonio, Texas dates back to the 1800's, although it is probable that ancient Indians created similar meals consisting of meat and chiles. Today's chili lovers feel very strongly about the contents of their chili. Arguments abound over the addition of vegetables. Purists believe only cubes of beef, chiles, onions and spices make up a real "bowl of red." Others believe the addition of beans and potatoes can only make a good thing better. Following are a selection of recipes for you to choose from.

✳ ✳ ✳ ✳ ✳

RED MESA CHILI

INGREDIENTS:

2 pounds beef stew meat
2 tablespoons oil
1 cup water
1 can green chiles, drained
2 cloves garlic, minced
1 teaspoon salt
1 tablespoon oil
1 onion, chopped fine
1 tablespoon flour
1 teaspoon oregano
1/4 teaspoon cumin
Water

Prepare meat by cutting into bite sized pieces and browning in 1 tablespoon oil. Add water and simmer for 1 hour, covered. Purée chiles in a blender with 1/2 cup broth from meat. Press purée through a sieve to remove bits of peel. Add purée to meat and broth. Mash garlic with salt to a paste. Cook garlic paste and onion in 1 tablespoon oil. Cook until onion is tender. Add flour and stir 1 minute. Add onion mixture, oregano and cumin to meat mixture. Simmer, covered, for 1 to 2 hours.
Serves 6.

✳ ✳ ✳ ✳ ✳

TEXAS CHILI

Big taste from the biggest state in the continental U.S.

INGREDIENTS:

2 pounds beef,
cut into bite size pieces
1 1/2 cups onion,
chopped
1 cup green
bell pepper, chopped
3 serrano chiles,
seeded and chopped
1 tablespoon oil
1/2 teaspoon garlic powder
2 tablespoons chili powder
1 teaspoon cumin
1 teaspoon oregano
1/2 teaspoon red pepper
1/3 cup masa
harina or cornmeal
1 16 ounce can stewed
tomatoes, undrained
1 can beef broth
1 can beer
1/3 teaspoon salt
1/2 teaspoon hot sauce
2 tablespoons lemon juice

In a heated skillet, cook meat until brown,
stirring often to prevent sticking. Drain and set aside.
Sauté onion, bell pepper and serrano chiles in oil until tender.
Add meat, chili powder, cumin, oregano, garlic and
red pepper. Sprinkle masa harina over meat mixture. Mix well.
Add tomatoes, beer, salt, hot sauce and beef broth and bring
to a boil. Simmer over medium heat for 1 1/2 hours.
Add lemon juice and simmer for 30 minutes
or until meat is tender.
Serves 6.

✳ ✳ ✳ ✳ ✳

Chili with Meatballs

INGREDIENTS:

1/2 pound ground pork
1 pound ground beef
1 green pepper,
chopped
2 medium onions,
chopped fine
2 tablespoons mild chili powder
1 12 oz can tomato paste
1 32 oz can kidney beans,
drained
1 24 oz can stewed tomatoes
Salt and pepper

In a large saucepan, or skillet, combine stewed tomatoes,
onions, green pepper, tomato paste, chili powder and salt
and pepper to taste. Bring to a boil. Simmer, covered,
for 2 hours, stirring often. Combine beef and pork and make
1 inch balls. Brown meatballs in a separate pan. Drain
excess oil and add to tomato mixture. Simmer on low heat
for 1 hour. Add beans and cook for 15 minutes.
Serves 6.

❋ ❋ ❋ ❋ ❋

Winchester Chili

INGREDIENTS:

2 pounds ground beef
1/2 cup chopped onion
1 1/4 cups canned tomatoes
4 cups canned kidney beans
1 teaspoon sugar
2 tablespoons chili powder

In a large skillet, brown beef and add onions, tomatoes,
beans, sugar and chili powder. Cover and cook slowly
for at least one hour. Top with grated Jack cheese
and serve with crackers or tortillas.
Serves 8.

CHACO CANYON CHILI

It's the wonderful selection of spices in this chili
that makes it so special. Add your own mix
of spices for a unique variation.

INGREDIENTS:

5 medium onions, chopped
1/4 teaspoon seasoning salt
1/4 teaspoon pepper
4 pounds ground beef
5 cloves garlic, minced
1 tablespoon oregano
2 teaspoons woodruff
1 teaspoon cayenne pepper
2 tablespoons paprika
3 tablespoons cumin powder
3 teaspoons oregano
2 teaspoons chili powder
1 teaspoon Tabasco sauce
3 10 ounce cans tomato sauce
1 teaspoon tomato paste
3 tablespoons flour
Vegetable oil

Sauté onions in oil. Add salt and pepper. Place
onions in a large chili pot. Brown beef, using oil if
necessary. Add garlic and 1 tablespoon of oregano.
Add cooked meat to the onions in the chili pot.
Mix together woodruff, cayenne pepper, paprika,
cumin, chili powder, and remaining oregano.
Add spice mixture to chili pot. Add Tabasco sauce,
tomato sauce and tomato paste to chili pot. Add
enough water to cover meat. Simmer on low for
2 hours. Bring chili to a boil. To thicken, make a
paste by mixing a little water and flour. Stir in
paste, stirring constantly until desired
thickness is achieved.
Serves 8.

✳ ✳ ✳ ✳ ✳

PORK WITH PINEAPPLE STEW

Of all the recipes I've tried out on my family,
this is my brother-in-laws favorite.
He raves about it and I think you will, too.

INGREDIENTS:

3 pounds porkloin,
cut in chunks
1 large tomato,
peeled and chopped
1 cup onion,
chopped
1 cup beef stock
1/4 cup
dry sherry
1/3 cup
sliced pimento
2 cups
pineapple chunks,
with juice
1/2 teaspoon chili powder
2 tablespoons flour
Salt
Pepper

Brown meat in a large skillet until meat is browned
on all sides. Add the onion and cook for 5 minutes,
or until onion is tender. Add the pineapple with its juice,
beef stock, dry sherry, sliced pimento, tomato and chili
powder to the skillet. Mix well then bring to boil. Reduce
heat and simmer. Add salt and pepper to taste. Cover and
simmer for 1 1/2 hours, until meat is tender. Stir often
to prevent sticking. Approximately 1/2 hour before serving,
sprinkle flour over simmering sauce and stir until sauce
thickens. Serve in bowls by itself, or over rice.
Serves 8.

✳ ✳ ✳ ✳ ✳

STEWED CHICKEN

I love this recipe for its to-die-for flavor. The garlic
and vinegar mixture gives the chicken a subtle
flavor that tastes wonderful and unique.

INGREDIENTS:

1 3 to 4 lb
broiler-fryer
1/8 teaspoon
garlic powder
1/2 teaspoon salt
1/8 teaspoon pepper
3 tablespoons white vinegar
3 tablespoons oil
1 medium
onion, chopped
3 large tomatoes,
peeled and chopped
12 Spanish green olives
1/2 teaspoon oregano
1 teaspoon salt

Cut chicken in quarters, wash and pat dry. Mix garlic
with 1/2 teaspoon salt, pepper and vinegar. Rub mixture all
over chicken. Let stand for one hour before cooking.
Brown chicken quarters in a skillet using 3 tablespoons oil.
Place browned chicken in large pot. Add onion, tomatoes,
olives, capers, oregano and 1 teaspoon salt. Bring to a boil.
Cover and simmer on low heat for 1 hour, turning
chicken pieces often.
Serves 4.

✳ ✳ ✳ ✳ ✳

A WORD ABOUT PAPRIKA

Paprika is dried ground ripe bell pepper,
the mildest of all peppers.

✳ ✳ ✳ ✳ ✳

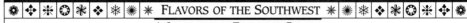
CHILI AND WHITE BEANS

INGREDIENTS:

3 pounds ground beef
1/2 pound dry navy
beans, rinsed
6 cups water
1 teaspoon
cumin powder
1/2 teaspoon
garlic powder
1 bay leaf
2 teaspoons salt
1 teaspoon oregano
2 tablespoons paprika
1 teaspoon brown sugar
1 tablespoon chili powder

Brown ground beef. Add water, bay leaf, garlic powder, salt, oregano, paprika, cumin powder, navy beans, brown sugar and chili powder. Cook over low heat for 3 hours uncovered and one hour covered.
Serves 6.

✳ ✳ ✳ ✳ ✳

CHILI STEW

INGREDIENTS:

· 1 quart cooked beans
2 tablespoons chili powder,
dissolved in 5 ounces water
2 tablespoons oil
Salt

Add oil to hot boiled beans. Salt to taste. Add dissolved chili powder. Simmer over medium-low heat for 45 minutes, stirring often.

✳ ✳ ✳ ✳ ✳

LAMB AND CHILE STEW

A more savory stew is hard to find!
Enjoy with warm tortillas.

INGREDIENTS:

2 lbs lamb, cut in cubes
1 medium onion, sliced
2 tablespoons oil
1/8 teaspoon garlic powder
1 16 oz can
plum tomatoes
1 celery stalk, chopped
1 1/2 cups corn,
fresh or frozen
1 7 oz can green chiles
1 cup beer
1 teaspoon oregano
1/2 teaspoon cumin
Salt
Pepper

Cook lamb in oil, browning on all sides. Remove
lamb from pan and reserve oil. Add onion, garlic
powder, celery and salt and pepper to taste in
reserved oil. Cook until tender. Mix in tomatoes,
corn, chiles, beer, oregano, cumin and lamb,
stirring often. Bring to a boil. Cover and simmer
on medium-low heat for 1 3/4 hours,
until meat is tender.
Serves 6.

✳ ✳ ✳ ✳ ✳

A WORD ABOUT CHILES:

Poblano chiles, dark green in color and slightly heart shaped,
become Ancho chiles when ripened and dried and
have a nice smoky flavor.

✳ ✳ ✳ ✳ ✳

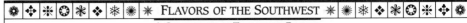
TURKEY MOLE POBLANO

INGREDIENTS:

1 8 oz jar mole poblano paste
3 cups diced cooked turkey
1 cup canned tomato sauce
1 cup chicken broth
Sugar
Salt

Blend mole paste, tomato sauce and stock in a large pot.
Bring to a boil and add sugar and salt to taste. Stir in
chicken and simmer on medium low heat for 15 minutes,
stirring often to blend flavors. To use as a tamale filling,
the sauce must be thick, so simmer until desired consistency.
Then spoon turkey pieces and sauce onto tamale dough
spread on corn husks. Use left over sauce to serve over cooked
tamales. Or Turkey Mole may be served as a stew or over rice.
Serves 4.

✳ ✳ ✳ ✳ ✳

TURKEY CHILI

INGREDIENTS:

1 pound coarsely ground turkey
3 tablespoons bacon drippings
1/2 cup onions, chopped
1 1/4 cups canned tomatoes
4 cups canned kidney beans
1 teaspoon seasoned salt
1 teaspoon sugar
2 tablespoons chili powder
1/4 cup Monterey Jack cheese,
shredded

Sauté onion in bacon drippings in a medium pot, draining
excess oil. Add ground turkey and cook until meat loses its
pink color. Add canned tomatoes, kidney beans, salt, sugar and
chili powder. Cover and simmer on low for 1 hour.
Garnish with cheese.
Serves 8.

Doctor's Chili

My optometrist, Dr. Terri Giese, was kind enough to contribute this recipe. She shows she can take care of your appetite as well as care for your eyes!

INGREDIENTS:

3 pounds ground
beef or turkey
2 cloves garlic, minced
2 medium onions,
chopped fine
1 green pepper, chopped fine
1 stalk celery, chopped fine
2 teaspoons oil
2 14 oz cans
stewed tomatoes,
undrained
1 15 ounce
can tomato sauce
1 6 ounce
can tomato paste
2 15 ounce cans of
kidney beans, drained
1/4 cup tomato/chili salsa
1 ounce chili powder
1 4 ounce can diced
green chiles, undrained
1/2 cup water
Salt
Pepper

In a dutch oven, sauté garlic, onions, pepper and celery in oil until tender. Add meat, one pound at a time. Stir over medium heat until meat loses red color. Drain. Add water, stewed tomatoes, tomato sauce, tomato paste, kidney beans, chili salsa, chili powder, and green chiles, stirring often. Simmer for 2 1/2 to 3 hours, stirring often. Add salt and pepper to taste.

✳ ✳ ✳ ✳ ✳

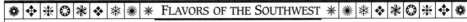

CHICKEN CHILI

This wonderful chili, also called White Chili because
chicken is used instead of beef, is a favorite
of chicken lovers everywhere.

INGREDIENTS:

1 1/2 cups onion, chopped
1/2 cup green
bell pepper, chopped
2 tablespoons oil
1 clove garlic,
minced
2 tablespoons
chili powder
2 tablespoons cumin
1 teaspoon oregano
4 cups cooked chicken meat,
cut in bite sized pieces
1 cup water
1/2 teaspoon
ground red pepper
1/4 teaspoon black pepper
1 tablespoon
Worcestershire sauce
1 tablespoon Dijon mustard
1 14 ounce
can stewed tomatoes
1 1/2 cups chicken broth
1 12 ounce bottle chili sauce
1 16 ounce can kidney beans
1 1/4 cups red onion, chopped
1 1/4 cups avocado,
peeled and diced

Sauté onion and bell pepper in oil until tender. Add garlic,
chili powder, oregano and cumin. Cook, stirring for 3 minutes.
Add chicken, 1 cup water, red pepper, black pepper,
Worcestershire sauce, mustard, tomatoes, chicken broth and
chili sauce. Bring to a boil. Cover and simmer over medium heat
for 20 minutes. Add beans and cook for 10 minutes.
Garnish each bowl with diced avocado and red onion.
Serves 8.

TOMATILLO CHILI

The combination of poblano chiles and tomatillos
gives this chili a wonderfully rich flavor.

INGREDIENTS:

1 1/4 pounds
ripe tomatillos,
peeled and seeded
6 poblano peppers
1 1/2 pounds pork,
cubed
1 cup onion,
chopped
1/2 teaspoon
garlic powder
2 teaspoons cumin
2 teaspoons oregano
1/2 cup cilantro,
chopped
1 tablespoon lemon juice
1/4 cup plain yogurt
Salt
Pepper

In a large pot cover tomatillos with water and bring
to a boil. Cook for 8 minutes, until tender. Drain,
reserving 1 cup fluid, and set aside. Brown
pork in a skillet, stirring often to brown evenly.
Remove meat from the skillet and, using remaining
oils, sauté peppers and onion. Cook for 5 minutes
before adding pork. Add tomatillos, reserved fluid,
cumin, garlic, oregano and salt and pepper,
stirring to mix. Bring mixture to a boil and
simmer on low heat for 5 minutes.
Top with a dollop of yogurt.
Serves 4.

✳ ✳ ✳ ✳ ✳

VEGETARIAN CHILI

This is another recipe contributed by my friend
Cathy Orlowski. She is a vegetarian who's natural
order of entertaining always involves fine food.

INGREDIENTS:

1 16 ounce can
pinto beans, drained
1 16 ounce can
kidney beans,
drained
9 cloves garlic,
unpeeled
8 large onions,
chopped
10 fresh mushrooms,
chopped fine
1 large zucchini,
chopped fine
1 28 oz can peeled
tomatoes, with fluid
4 tablespoons butter
1 1/2 teaspoons chili powder
1 teaspoon cumin
1/2 teaspoon cayenne pepper
1/2 cup Monterey Jack
cheese, shredded
Salt

Cover garlic cloves with water in a small saucepan and
cook over high heat until the water boils. Drain and
cool garlic for 5 minutes. Peel and chop. Sauté onions
in butter in a large pan until tender and light brown.
Add garlic and sauté for 5 minutes. Add zucchini and
mushrooms and sauté until tender. Add tomatoes with fluid,
chili powder, cumin, cayenne pepper and salt to taste. Bring
mixture to a boil. Simmer over medium heat for 50 minutes.
Add kidney and pinto beans and cook for 30 minutes.
Garnish each serving with shredded Jack cheese.
Serves 6.

✳ ✳ ✳ ✳ ✳

BEEF AND VEGETABLE CHILI

It's the extra vegetables and spices that give this
chili its special flavor. Serve with chile corn
bread and a glass of sangria or Sun Tea.

INGREDIENTS:

3 pounds ground beef
1 cup onions, chopped
1 green pepper, chopped
2 stalks celery, chopped
2 carrots, chopped
1 cucumber, chopped
1 zucchini, chopped
1/8 teaspoon garlic powder
1 10 ounce can of tomato sauce
1 16 ounce can of tomatoes,
chopped
1 16 ounce can pinto beans
1/2 teaspoon parsley
1/4 teaspoon saffron
1/4 teaspoon rosemary
1 teaspoon salt
1/2 teaspoon pepper
1 tablespoon Tabasco sauce

In a large pan cook beef, onions, green peppers, celery,
carrots, cucumber, zucchini, and garlic powder until
vegetables become tender. Simmer over low heat for
1 hour. Add tomato sauce, chopped tomatoes,
pinto beans, parsley, saffron, rosemary, salt and pepper
and Tabasco sauce. Cook for 3 hours adding water
for desired consistency.
Serves 6.

✳ ✳ ✳ ✳ ✳

MEXICAN PORK CHILI

INGREDIENTS:

3 1/2 pounds boneless pork,
cut in bite sized cubes
4 medium tomatoes,
quartered
2 7 oz cans green
chiles, cut in strips
1 large onion, chopped
2 cloves garlic, minced
1 teaspoon oregano
1/4 teaspoon cumin
1 teaspoon salt

Place pork in a large pot and cover with water. Bring to a boil
and let simmer over reduced heat for 40 minutes. Drain pork
and place in a large skillet. Brown the meat and remove
any fat. Add onions and garlic and cook until onions become
tender. Add tomatoes, chiles, oregano, cumin and salt.
Cover skillet and cook over medium heat for about 10 minutes.
Uncover and continue cooking for 20 minutes.
Serves 6.

❋ ❋ ❋ ❋ ❋

TERESA'S TERRIFIC CHILI

INGREDIENTS:

1 1/2 pounds ground turkey
1 cup cooked pinto beans
1/2 cup green pepper
4 tablespoons green chile, diced
4 3/4 cups canned tomatoes,
crushed and drained
2 tablespoons chili powder

Brown ground turkey. Add onions and pepper and cook until
peppers are tender. Add beans, chile, tomatoes and chili powder
and mix well. Simmer over low heat for 35 minutes.
Serves 4.

ABSOLUTELY FABULOUS CHILI

INGREDIENTS:

1 pound beef tenderloin, cubed
2 cloves garlic, chopped
1 onion, chopped
1 tablespoon oil
1 teaspoon oregano
1 cup tomato sauce
1 cup kidney beans
1 cup water
Salt and pepper

Brown beef and set aside. Saute onion and garlic in oil until tender. Add meat, oregano, tomato sauce, and kidney beans. Add water and salt and pepper to taste. Bring to a boil and let simmer slowly for 1 to 2 hours, until meat becomes tender. Add more water if necessary.
Serves 4.

✳ ✳ ✳ ✳ ✳

LUCIA'S LUSCIOUS CHILI

INGREDIENTS:

1 pound lean ground beef
1/2 cup celery, chopped fine
1 small onion, chopped fine
2 cloves garlic, minced
1 15 ounce can tomato sauce
1 tablespoon chili powder
Salt and pepper

Cook ground beef, celery, onion and garlic until beef turns brown. Drain excess fat. Add tomato sauce, chili powder and salt and pepper to taste. Simmer over medium heat for 25 minutes or until desired thickness is achieved.
Serves 4.

✳ ✳ ✳ ✳ ✳

MEXICAN STEW

A tender beef stew that whets your taste buds
and sticks to your ribs. A special treat for
anyone with a hearty appetite.

INGREDIENTS:

2 pounds beef shank
3 quarts water
3/4 teaspoon
garlic powder
1 medium
onion, sliced
10 peppercorns
6 tablespoons
tomato puree
2 large potatoes,
peeled and cubed
3 ears of corn,
cut in 1 inch pieces
3 cups green beans,
cut into 1 inch pieces
4 medium zucchini, sliced
3 large carrots, peeled and
cut in 1 inch pieces
1 tablespoon salt

Brown shanks in a 450°F oven. Combine browned
beef, drippings, water, garlic powder, peppercorns,
onion and salt in a large pot. Bring to a boil.
Cover and cook on low for 2 hours, or until meat
is tender. Remove meat. Strain broth and return to pot.
Add tomato purée and bring to a boil. Add vegetables
and cook on low for 30 minutes or until vegetables
are tender. Remove meat from bone and add to soup.
Cook long enough to heat meat and serve.
Serves 8.

✻ ✻ ✻ ✻ ✻

VALLEY OF THE SUN CHILI

A popular chili here in Phoenix and surrounding
areas of the spectacular Valley of the Sun.

INGREDIENTS:

4 pounds beef steak,
cut in slices
2 12 ounce
cans tomato sauce
1 12 ounce can of water
5 large onions,
chopped
2 bell peppers
1 can cola drink
9 tablespoons
chili powder
1 tablespoon oregano
1 tablespoon sugar
1 tablespoon pepper
1 tablespoon salt
1/2 teaspoon cilantro
1/4 cup oil

Mix cola with chili powder, sugar, oregano,
pepper, salt and cilantro. and set aside.
Heat oil in a skillet and sautée onions until
tender. Remove to a large pot. Discard excess oil
and using the same pan, brown the beef steak.
Place the steak in the large pot with onions.
Mix the spice mixture with tomato sauce and water
and stir into pot. Simmer for 3 hours, stirring often.
When meat becomes tender add salt and pepper
to taste and place in the refrigerator for
3 hours. Reheat and add lime juice
when ready to serve.
Serves 6.

✳ ✳ ✳ ✳ ✳

BEEF STEW

This is a hearty beef, bean and vegetable stew
that will be sure to satisfy even the biggest
appetites. Serve with a chunk of corn
bread and a tall glass of milk
or your favorite cerveza.

INGREDIENTS:

4 chicken breasts
1 3 pound
chuck roast
2 cups navy beans
3 cups water
1/4 cup olive oil
2 medium onions
4 medium potatoes
4 large carrots
4 medium parsnips
3 peppercorns
Croutons
Salt
Pepper

Cover and soak beans overnight. Drain.
In a large Dutch Oven, heat oil and add chicken
and chuck roast. Fry both until completely brown.
Add beans to the Dutch Oven and add enough
water to cover meat and beans. Bring to a boil.
Simmer for 3 hours. As meat and beans simmer, slice
vegetables then add, with spices, to stew. Cook
over medium low heat for 1 1/2 hours, or until meat
is tender. Remove vegetables and meat from mixture.
To serve, pour broth into soup bowls and garnish
with croutons. Serve meat and vegetables together.
Serves 6.

✳ ✳ ✳ ✳ ✳

MENUDO

This tripe and chile stew is a traditional Mexican dish that is widely thought to be a cure for the average hang-over. Give it a try and see for yourself.

INGREDIENTS:

2 pounds tripe,
cut into 1 inch squares
2 gallons water
1 tablespoon salt
1 cup green onion,
sliced
1/2 hot red chile
pepper, ground
2 green peppers,
sliced with seeds
1/3 cup parsley
2 tomatoes,
cut in half
Salt

Place tripe in large pot and cover with 1 gallon of water. Bring to a boil. Mix 1 gallon of water with salt and bring to a boil. Drain tripe and cover with salty water. Keep on low boil for 2 hours. Add green onion, chile pepper, green peppers and parsley. Simmer for 1 1/2 hours on low heat. Add tomatoes and simmer for another 30 minutes. Serves 8.

✳ ✳ ✳ ✳ ✳

A WORD ABOUT MEAT:

The nutritional, and according to many people, medicinal, Tripe is the stomach lining of cattle or other ruminants.

✳ ✳ ✳ ✳ ✳

GREEN CHILE STEW

The unique flavor of this spicy stew makes it a
Mexican favorite. A meal in itself when served
over Mexican rice and with corn tortillas.

INGREDIENTS:

2 pounds
boneless pork butt
1 medium onion,
chopped
1 clove garlic, minced
2 teaspoons flour
1 8 1/4 ounce
can whole tomatoes
1 7 oz. can
chopped green chiles
1 10 ounce can tomatoes
with hot green chiles
Salt
Pepper

Trim fat from pork butt and cut into 1 inch cubes.
In a large skillet, brown pork and add onion
and garlic. Cook until tender and stir in flour.
Cook for 2 minutes, stirring. Add whole tomatoes,
chiles and tomatoes with hot chiles. Cut up
tomatoes with a fork and continue stirring. Salt and
pepper to taste. Simmer on low for 1 to 2 hours,
or until meat is tender. Garnish with parsley.
Serves 4.

✳ ✳ ✳ ✳ ✳

BEER CHILI

Cooking with beer probably started when a cook had
too many cervezas and decided to share one.
The alcohol cooks out but a special flavor remains.

INGREDIENTS:

4 pounds ground beef
3 onions, chopped
1 teaspoon cumin powder
1/8 teaspoon garlic powder
1 12 ounce can tomatoes
1 teaspoon sugar
1/2 can
Mexican beer
2 packs chili seasoning
1 tablespoon
Tabasco sauce
1 quart water
4 jalapeño peppers,
chopped
Salt
Pepper

Brown ground beef thoroughly. Add onion, cumin
powder, garlic powder and salt and pepper to taste.
Mix in tomatoes, sugar, beer, chili seasoning,
chili powder, Tabasco sauce, water and peppers.
Cook on low for 3 hours, uncovered.
Serves 8.

✳ ✳ ✳ ✳ ✳

MAIN DISHES
SOUTHWESTERN FAVORITES

In this chapter you will find many traditional
Southwestern dishes that have been updated to reflect
the essence of the new Southwest. Also featured are many
recipes created by newcomers who have brought family
recipes and their own regional specialties which have
become the new favorites of the Southwest. My personal
favorites include the *Chicken Chile Cheeseburger*, the
very savory *Taos Pork* and a *Chile Fettuccine*
that simply melts in your mouth. Enjoy!

MARINATED SIRLOIN STEAK

INGREDIENTS:

1 cup olive oil
2 pounds
sirloin steak, trimmed
2 tablespoons dry mustard
2 tablespoons
Worcestershire sauce
2 cloves garlic, minced
1 teaspoon soy sauce
1/4 teaspoon
Tabasco sauce
1 tablespoon
fresh lime juice
Salt and pepper

Combine olive oil, reserving 2 tablespoons, dry mustard,
Worcestershire sauce, garlic, soy sauce, Tabasco sauce, lime
juice and salt and pepper to taste. Pour mixture over meat,
which has been placed in a glass container, and refrigerate
overnight. Turn meat often. Preheat oven to 375°F. Two
hours before roasting, remove meat from refrigerator and
bring meat to room temperature. Using reserved oil, sear
meat on both sides in a very hot skillet and then place
in oven to cook until a meat thermometer reads 135°F.
Slice and serve with pan drippings as sauce.
Serves 6.

SHREDDED BEEF BURRITOS

Burritos can be made with almost anything and are
always a great way to use left over meat, poultry or fish.

INGREDIENTS:

1 pound beef stew meat
1 1/2 cups water
Salt and pepper to taste
1/2 onion, chopped
1 clove garlic, minced
2 tablespoons oil
3 medium tomatoes,
peeled and chopped
1 green pepper,
chopped
1 tablespoon
chili powder
4 large flour tortillas
1 1/2 cups refried beans
1 1/2 cups Monterey or
Cheddar cheese, shredded
Shredded lettuce
Salsa

Combine beef, water and salt and pepper to taste
in a large pot. Bring to a boil and simmer, covered,
on low heat for about 2 hours, or until beef is tender.
Set aside to cool. Once meat is cool enough, drain and
reserve broth. Shred meat with a fork. In medium skillet,
sauté onion and garlic in oil until tender. Add tomatoes
and simmer for 10 minutes. Add green pepper, chili
powder and shredded meat. Add 1/2 cup broth and
salt and pepper again to taste. Simmer on low for
15 minutes, until green pepper is tender. Heat refried
beans and spread a couple of tablespoons of beans on
flour tortilla, add shredded beef, cheese, lettuce and
salsa. Fold bottom of tortilla up, about 3 inches, then
fold left or right side over and roll to finish. Serve on
shredded lettuce and top with cheese. Serve
with red or green sauce if desired.
Serves 4.

FLAT ENCHILADAS

INGREDIENTS:

1/2 cup dried pinto beans
1 medium onion, quartered
2 cloves garlic
1/2 teaspoon salt
1 1.3 pound can
enchilada sauce
2 tablespoons oil
1 pound ground beef
1/2 teaspoon oregano
1/2 teaspoon cumin
2 cups mild Cheddar
cheese, shredded
1/2 cup oil
12 corn tortillas
1 avocado, sliced thin
3/4 cup sour cream
4 cups lettuce, shredded
12 ripe olives, pitted
2 tomatoes, cut in wedges

Rinse beans and cover with hot water. Let stand
overnight. Drain and rinse. Add 1/8 onion and 1 clove
garlic. Cover with water and bring to a boil. Simmer
on low heat for 2 hours. Add 1/2 teaspoon salt and
simmer for 2 hours, or until beans are tender. Heat
enchilada sauce. Chop remaining onion, mince last
clove garlic. Scramble and cook ground beef to a light
brown. Add onion and garlic. Cook until onion is tender.
Add 1 1/4 cups enchilada sauce, oregano and cumin.
Add beans and simmer on low for 5 minutes. Add salt to
taste. Prepare enchiladas on ovenproof plate. Divide cheese
into 4 servings. Preheat oven to 350°F. In heated oil, soften
a tortilla for 3 or 4 seconds on each side. Place over paper
towels to absorb the extra oil. Place on plate and cover with
1/3 cup meat mixture and some cheese. Repeat process until
there are 3 layers of tortillas, meat and cheese. Cover top
with 1/4 cup enchilada sauce. Prepare 3 more enchiladas.
Bake for 10 minutes or until cheese is melted. Arrange
avocado and tomato wedges in pattern on top of
enchiladas. Top with sour cream and olives.
Serves 4.

HIGH DESERT POT ROAST

This is unlike any pot roast I've ever had before.
The brown sugar, wine vinegar and chiles
really make it flavorful.

INGREDIENTS:

3 pounds
beef chuck steak
1 1/4 cups
dry white wine
4 tablespoons
wine vinegar
5 green chiles,
cleaned, chopped
4 tablespoons
brown sugar
2 teaspoons salt
2 cloves garlic,
minced
1 onion, chopped
3/4 cup beef broth
3 tablespoons butter
3 tablespoons tomato paste

Combine white wine, wine vinegar, chiles,
brown sugar, salt and garlic, mix well. Place
beef in a shallow pan and pour marinade over.
Cover and refrigerate overnight, turning several
times. When you are ready to cook, drain beef and
reserve marinade. In a large skillet, brown beef in
butter on both sides. Add 1 to 2 cups of marinade,
onion, broth and tomato paste. Cover and simmer
for 1 1/2 hours, or until the beef is very tender.
Simmer, uncovered, for 1/2 hour to allow
sauce to thicken. Serve pot roast sliced,
with sauce served separately.
Serves 8.

BARE CHILE RELLENOS

There are many ways to fill a chile and this is only
one of several good recipes found in this chapter.

INGREDIENTS FOR MARINADE:

1 7 ounce can
whole green chiles
1/3 cup olive oil
3 tablespoons wine vinegar
1/8 teaspoon garlic powder
Pepper
Salt

INGREDIENTS FOR FILLING:

7 ounces
cooked chicken
1 medium potato, cubed
1 medium carrot, cubed
1/4 medium onion, diced
1 tablespoon parsley
1 Tbsp cilantro
1/3 cup mayonnaise
3 Tbsp sour cream

In a shallow pan combine olive oil, wine vinegar, garlic
powder, salt and pepper to taste. Peel and seed chiles, leaving
stem and chile whole. Cut a slit down the side of each chile
and place in the marinade for 2 1/2 hours. Cook the diced carrot
and potato in enough water to cover for 8 to 10 minutes or
until tender. Cut cooked chicken into bite sized squares and
add potatoes, carrots, parsley, onion, cilantro, sour cream,
mayonnaise and 3 tablespoons marinade. Salt and pepper to
taste. Remove chiles from marinade and place on paper
towels to drain excess marinade. Fill each chile with chicken
mixture. Garnish with sour cream or parsley and serve.
Serves 6.

TAMALE CASSEROLE

INGREDIENTS:

1 medium onion, chopped
1 pound ground beef
2 cups canned tomatoes
2 cups cream corn
1 cup milk
2 tablespoons oil
1 cup cornmeal, uncooked
2 teaspoons salt
1 teaspoon pepper
2 tablespoons chili powder
1/2 pound Monterey
Jack cheese, grated

Heat oil in heavy skillet and cook onion until tender. Add ground beef and brown. Add tomatoes, corn, milk, cornmeal, chili powder, salt and pepper and mix well. Spread grated cheese evenly over mixture and cook on stovetop for 25 minutes. Serves 8.

BURRITOS

INGREDIENTS:

3 1/2 cups refried beans
15 flour tortillas, warmed
1 1/2 cups ground beef filling
1/2 onion, chopped
Cheddar Cheese

Lay one tortilla on a plate and place 4 tablespoons refried beans in the middle. Spread beans evenly over tortilla, leaving about 1 inch uncovered around edges. Spoon 1 heaping tablespoon beef filling over 1/2 of beans, leaving edges of tortilla uncovered. Sprinkle chopped onion and cheese as desired. Fold tortilla by folding sides of tortilla until outer edges meet in the middle. Roll from the bottom of the tortilla until completely rolled. Serve with the seam down. Serves 15.

TAOS PORK

This zesty pork dish must be experienced to be believed.

INGREDIENTS:

2 pounds pork,
trimmed and cubed
1 tablespoon chili powder
2 10 ounce
cans enchilada sauce
2 cups water
2 tablespoons flour
1/2 teaspoon cumin
2 cloves garlic, minced
1 teaspoon sugar
1 teaspoon salt
1 teaspoon pepper

In a large skillet, cook pork until lightly browned. Add chili
powder and flour. Mix well. Add enchilada sauce, water,
cumin, garlic, sugar, salt and pepper and bring to a boil.
Simmer, for 1 1/2 to 2 hours. Add water to thin, if desired.
Serves 6.

CHILE BURGERS

INGREDIENTS:

1 pound lean ground beef
2 7 oz cans of whole green chiles,
seeded, deveined and chopped
Whole wheat hamburger buns
Salt and pepper
Salsa

Combine ground beef and chopped chiles and form into
burgers. Salt and pepper burgers before grilling to desired
doneness. Place burger on bottom bun and spoon a small
amount of salsa on top of burger before topping with bun.
Serves 6.

CHEESE ENCHILADAS

This excellent combination of cheese, tortillas and
sauce makes a simple but filling meal.

INGREDIENTS:

1 cup Cheddar cheese,
shredded
2 1/3 cup
canned Enchilada Sauce
1 cup Monterey Jack
cheese, shredded
6 corn tortillas
1 small onion,
chopped
3 green onions,
chopped
1/4 cup oil

Heat enchilada sauce in pan. Mix cheeses and set aside.
Fry tortillas, one at a time, in hot oil for 3 to 5 seconds
per side. Drain on paper towels and immediately dip
in heated sauce. Place tortilla on a plate and spread
cheese in a line just below the center. Lightly spread
chopped onion over cheese. Roll tortilla tightly and place
seam down in a shallow baking dish. Repeat with
each tortilla, saving 1/3 of the cheese to use as topping.
When all enchiladas are prepared, cover with left over
sauce and top with cheese. Bake 15 to 20 minutes.
Garnish with green onions and serve hot.

A WORD ABOUT INGREDIENTS:

Corn husks, used in the preparation of tamales, are sold
by the package and can be found in Mexican markets and
many well-stocked grocery stores in the Southwest.
To use, soften corn husks in warm
water for 2 to 3 hours. Discard any
miscellaneous pieces of silk.

MEAT FILLINGS

There are many ways to fill tacos,
bell peppers, tamales and even whole
California chiles. For easy entertaining,
prepare fillings in advance and freeze.
The filling recipes that follow offer
a variety of delightful tastes.

SHREDDED BEEF

INGREDIENTS:

1/2 medium onion,
sliced thin
1 pound
beef stew meat
1 tablespoon chili powder
1 clove garlic, minced
1 1/2 cups water
2 tablespoons oil
3 medium tomatoes,
peeled and chopped

Combine beef, water and salt to taste in large pot.
Bring to a boil. Simmer, covered, on low heat for
1 3/4 hours, or until beef is tender. Set aside to
cool. Drain and reserve broth. Shred meat with
a fork. Sauté onion and garlic until tender. Add
tomatoes and simmer for 10 minutes. Stir in
green pepper, chili powder and meat. Add
1/2 cup broth and salt and pepper to taste.
Simmer on low for 15 minutes, until
green pepper becomes tender.

CHICKEN FILLING

INGREDIENTS:

2 cups shredded chicken
2/3 cup canned enchilada sauce
1 small canned
jalapeño chile, chopped
1 medium onion,
chopped
1/4 cup raisins
2 tablespoons oil
Salt and pepper

Cook onion in oil until tender, add chicken, enchilada sauce, chile and raisins. Simmer for 10 minutes, stirring often. Salt and pepper to taste.

CRAB FILLING

INGREDIENTS:

6 ozs canned crab,
drained
1 tablespoon raisins,
plumped in hot water,
drained
1 tablespoon almonds,
chopped
1 tablespoon parsley,
chopped
1 tablespoon oil
1 clove garlic, minced
1/2 medium onion, chopped
1 teaspoon capers
Salt and pepper to taste

Sauté onion and garlic in hot oil. Add flaked crab, raisins, and capers. Mix well. Cook over medium heat for 4 minutes. Fills 6 tacos or enchiladas.

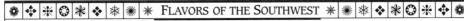
MINCED MEAT FILLING

INGREDIENTS:

1/2 pound ground beef
1/2 pound ground pork
1/2 small onion, chopped
1/4 teaspoon garlic powder
2 teaspoons capers
2 tablespoons parsley
1 medium tomato,
peeled and chopped
2 tablespoons
blanched almonds, chopped
2 tablespoons raisins,
soaked in hot water until soft

Cook and scramble beef and pork until light brown.
Drain excess oil. Add onion, tomato, garlic, capers, almonds,
and raisins. Cook over medium heat for 10 minutes,
stirring often. Salt to taste.

HAMBURGER FILLING

INGREDIENTS:

1 pound ground beef
1 medium onion, chopped
1/2 cup canned enchilada sauce
Pepper
Salt
Oil

Scramble and brown meat, adding oil if necessary.
Add onion and cook until tender. Mix in enchilada sauce
and simmer, covered, for 15 minutes.
Salt and pepper to taste.
Fills 6 to 8 tacos.

CHORIZO FILLING

Often served at breakfast with eggs, chorizo is a spicy
Mexican sausage that can be made ahead of time
and successfully frozen for future use.

INGREDIENTS:

1 1/2 pounds pork,
finely ground
1 onion, chopped
2 cloves garlic
2 teaspoons
chili powder
1 teaspoon oregano
1/2 teaspoon cumin
1/2 teaspoon
each salt and pepper
3 tablespoons vinegar

Combine onion, garlic, chili powder, oregano, cumin,
salt and pepper into a food processor and process until
smooth. Add vinegar and process until smooth. Add spice
mixture to ground pork and mix, using your hands.
When pork and spices have been mixed well, cover and
refrigerate for at least one day to allow flavors to blend.
Shape chorizo into patties or cook scrambled.

A WORD ABOUT INGREDIENTS:

Chorizo can also be purchased at the
grocery store, and is often sold by the pound.

Garlic was revered by both the Ancient Egyptians and
Romans who used it to strengthen their soldiers for battle.
Garlic was also considered to be protection against the ever
present vampires and werewolves of ancient times.

RED WINE LAMB

Yes, this takes time to prepare but when it's done
and you're ready to dig into this delicious meal,
you won't mind the effort.

INGREDIENTS:

4 pounds lamb shanks
3 dried California chiles
3 dried pasilla negro chiles
1 cup red wine
1/4 teaspoon ginger
1/2 teaspoon
garlic powder
1 teaspoon cumin
1 teaspoon oregano
1/2 teaspoon salt
1/2 teaspoon pepper
1/8 teaspoon chili powder
Water

In a large saucepan, cover California and pasilla
negro chiles with water. Bring to a boil and let stand
until softened, about 45 minutes. Drain and clean
discarding stems and seeds. In a blender, purée
softened chiles, wine, ginger, garlic, cumin, oregano,
chili powder and salt and pepper. Press mixture through
a sieve to remove bits of peel. Place lamb shanks in
a baking dish and coat with chile mixture. Cover
and let sit in refrigerator for 5 hours, or overnight.
Remove from refrigerator and bring to room
temperature before cooking. Preheat oven to
350°F. Cover dish with foil and bake for 2 hours,
or until tender. Turn meat in marinade every hour,
making sure to recover with foil. Let cool. Serve
on the bone with a five bean salad, or remove
the meat from the bones, discarding bones,
and serving with greens and chiles.
Serves 6.

MEXICAN HASH

This recipe is so versatile you can throw in
almost anything. It makes a great meal
from scratch or utilizes leftovers.

INGREDIENTS:

1 pound ground pork
1 pound ground beef
1 large onion, chopped
1/4 teaspoon garlic powder
2 medium tomatoes,
peeled, seeded and chopped
1 Granny Smith
apple, peeled and grated
1 tablespoon sugar
1/4 cup beef broth
4 tablespoons almond slivers
3 tablespoons black
olives, pitted and chopped
2 tablespoons chili powder
1/4 teaspoon cinnamon
1/4 teaspoon cumin
1 tablespoon vinegar
1/4 cup raisins,
softened in warm water
1/2 teaspoon oregano
Pepper
Salt

In a large skillet, cook pork, beef and onion until
meat begins to brown. Add the tomatoes and beef
broth and mix well. Simmer for 15 minutes before adding
garlic powder, tomatoes, sugar, almonds, black olives,
chili powder, cinnamon, cumin, vinegar, oregano and
raisins. Bring to a boil. Add apples and simmer
over medium low heat for 1/2 hour, stirring often.
Serve with a side of refried beans and corn bread.
Serves 8.

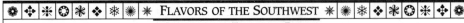
TOMATO AND PEPPER PORK CHOPS

This is another very easy to prepare dish that gives the impression of much time spent in the kitchen.

INGREDIENTS:

6 pork chops
1 tablespoon oil
7 medium tomatoes, chopped
3 green peppers, chopped
2 tablespoons flour
Salt and pepper

Sift the flour, salt and pepper to taste. Coat pork chops with flour mixture and brown in a skillet. Add tomatoes and peppers and cover. Simmer for 25 minutes.
Serves 6.

BAKED PORKLOIN

INGREDIENTS:

1 3 pound porkloin roast
1 tablespoon chili powder
2 cloves garlic
1/2 teaspoon oregano
1 16 oz bottle of Coca Cola
Salt and pepper to taste

Preheat oven to 350°F. Mix chili powder, garlic, oregano and 1/4 bottle of cola in a blender or food processor. Salt and pepper the pork roast evenly. Brown all sides of pork roast in a skillet. Drain excess oils from meat and put into a baking pan. Spread cola mixture over meat. Add remaining cola to meat and place in preheated oven. Bake for 2 hours, or until a meat thermometer reaches 170°F. Baste often with pan mixture. Serve pan fluid as sauce when serving meat.
Serves 6.

ZUCCHINI AND CHILE CASSEROLE

This savory casserole can be served as a side dish or as a meal all by itself when served with warm tortillas or French bread.

INGREDIENTS:

4 cups zucchini,
sliced
1 onion, chopped
1 clove garlic, minced
1/2 cup canned green
chiles, drained and chopped
1/2 cup canned cream corn
2 tablespoons butter
2 tablespoons hot water
1 cup Cheddar
cheese, shredded
4 eggs, beaten
1 tablespoon fresh
parsley, chopped
Salt
Pepper

Preheat oven to 350°F. Grease a 1 to 2 quart casserole dish. In a medium skillet, sauté onion in butter until tender. Add zucchini, garlic, chiles and water. Reduce heat and cook for about 7 minutes, or until zucchini is tender, stirring often to prevent sticking. Add corn, 1/2 cup cheese, eggs, parsley and salt and pepper to taste. Place zucchini and chile mixture in casserole dish and top with remaining cheese. Bake for 45 minutes or until set. Serves 6.

TACOS

Tacos are simply tortilla sandwiches, an easy way to eat without a mess. Use chicken, beef, pork or vegetables as fillers if you choose.

INGREDIENTS:

1 pound ground beef
1 1/2 teaspoons
chili powder
1 medium
onion, chopped fine
1/2 teaspoon oregano
1/2 teaspoon paprika
1/4 teaspoon garlic salt
2 teaspoons
Worcestershire
1/4 teaspoon rosemary
1/4 teaspoon cumin
12 corn tortillas,
fried and folded
1 cup Cheddar
cheese, shredded
1 head
lettuce, shredded

Scramble meat in a skillet and cook until brown. Add onion and chili powder, oregano, paprika, cumin, rosemary, garlic salt, pepper, and Worcestershire sauce. Simmer for 15 minutes on low, stirring occasionally. Fill folded tortilla with taco meat, lettuce, cheese, tomatoes and top with your choice of taco sauce. For a soft taco, spoon filling slightly off center of tortilla and fold.
Makes 12 tacos.

STUFFED PEPPERS

This is a very simple and light meal that can be attractively presented by slicing the pepper in half lengthwise, without disturbing the stem, and filling.

INGREDIENTS:

4 red or green peppers,
cored and seeded
2 cups
chicken stock

INGREDIENTS FOR STUFFING:

2 onions, sliced
2 tablespoons butter
1/4 pound
mushrooms, chopped
2 cups cooked rice
2 tablespoons
parsley, chopped
1 teaspoon oregano
Salt
Pepper

Preheat oven to 350°F. To prepare stuffing, sauté onion in butter until tender. Add mushrooms, cooked rice, parsley, oregano and salt and pepper to taste. Cook for 5 minutes. Place peppers in a deep baking dish and fill with stuffing. Pour stock over top and bake for 45 minutes to an hour, until tender. Serves 4.

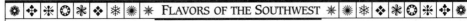

TENDERLOIN WITH BLACK BEAN RELISH

A favorite dish of both Norte-Americanos and Mexicans, this Pork Tenderloin is easy to make yet elegant enough to serve to unexpected guests.

INGREDIENTS:

1 tablespoon oil
2 cloves garlic, crushed
1 pound
pork tenderloin
1 tablespoon
oregano, chopped
1 medium tomato,
chopped fine
1/4 cup green onions,
sliced
1 teaspoon oregano,
chopped
1/2 teaspoon ground cumin
1/4 teaspoon salt
1/4 teaspoon pepper
1 16 ounce can black beans,
drained and rinsed

Preheat oven to 325°F. Combine oil and garlic and brush over tenderloin. Spread 1 tablespoon oregano over tenderloin. Place roast in a shallow pan. Roast for 45 minutes or until a meat thermometer reads 170°F. Remove meat from oven. Combine chopped tomato, green onions, oregano, cumin, salt, pepper and black beans. Cook over medium heat until heated through, stirring often. To serve, slice tenderloin on the diagonal and dish hot relish over top.
Serves 4.

GREEN CHILE
MEAT LOAF

This recipe proves that meat loaf does not have to be
the same as the one your mother used to make.
The chiles add a zing to an old favorite.

INGREDIENTS:

1 1/2 pounds
lean ground beef
1 cup canned
tomatoes, undrained
1 4 ounce
can green chiles,
seeded and chopped
1 cup soft bread crumbs
3 tablespoons
dried onion flakes
1 1/2 teaspoon salt
1/4 teaspoon garlic salt

Preheat oven to 375°F. Combine ground beef,
tomatoes, chiles, bread crumbs, onion flakes,
salt and garlic salt. Mix well, using your hands.
Place mixture in a large loaf pan and press
lightly. Bake for 1 hour. Cover with
enchilada sauce if desired.
Serves 6.

A WORD ABOUT TEQUILA:

Tequila is made from the maguey, a succulent plant
that is quite large and has long, thick leaves.
Premium tequila is aged in oak casks and
has a beautiful golden color.

CREAM CHEESE ENCHILADAS

A unique recipe contributed by Dr. Terri Giese, a
Scottsdale optometrist with a talent in the kitchen.

INGREDIENTS:

1 5 ounce
can cooked chicken
1 4 ounce can
green chiles, sliced
1 8 ounce package
cream cheese, sliced thin
12 corn tortillas
1 12 ounce
can enchilada sauce
2 cups Monterey
Jack cheese, shredded
1/4 cup oil

Preheat oven to 350°F. Pour enchilada sauce in a
shallow dish. Heat oil in a skillet and cook tortillas for
30 seconds. Remove tortillas from oil and dip in
enchilada sauce. Place 2 tablespoons chicken, slice of
cream cheese and chiles just off center of tortilla and roll.
Place rolled enchiladas in a 9x13 inch baking dish and pour
remaining enchilada sauce over all. Spread shredded
cheese on top and bake for 20 minutes,
until cheese has melted.

A WORD ABOUT CHEESE:

Cheese should always be wrapped tightly to prevent moisture
loss and to maintain texture. Unripened cheeses, like
cottage and cream cheese, have a higher water
content and are more perishable than
hard cheese. Use cream cheese
within two weeks
of purchase.

VERACRUZ ENCHILADAS

The crab filling, with its capers, almonds
and raisins, gives this dish its style.

INGREDIENTS:

1 tablespoon
parsley, chopped
1 tablespoon
almonds, chopped
1 19 ounce
can enchilada sauce
1/4 cup oil
6 corn tortillas
Sour cream
6 ounces canned crab, drained
1 tablespoon raisins,
plumped in hot water, drained
1 tablespoon
almonds, chopped
1 tablespoon
parsley, chopped
1 tablespoon oil
1 clove garlic, minced
1/2 medium onion, chopped
1 teaspoon capers
Salt and pepper to taste

To prepare crab filling, sauté onion and garlic in hot
oil. Add flaked crab, raisins, and capers. Mix well.
Cook over medium heat for 4 minutes. Preheat oven
to 350°F. Warm enchilada sauce. Fry tortillas, one at a
time, in hot oil for 3 to 5 seconds, each side. Drain
over paper towels to absorb excess oil. Spoon a
generous amount of crab filling on each tortilla. Roll
and place in baking dish. After all tortillas are filled
and rolled, cover with enchilada sauce. Place foil over
baking dish and bake for 15 to 20 minutes. Garnish
with sour cream, parsley and almonds.
Serves 6.

LAMB WITH CHILE SAUCE

An excellent lamb dish, and the chile sauce can be used on beef and chicken as well. Grill on the barbeque to get a smokey flavor.

INGREDIENTS:

5 pound leg of
lamb, boned and
flattened
1/3 cup olive oil
1 teaspoon salt
1 teaspoon pepper
2 medium onions, diced
2 cups chili sauce
1/2 cup lemon juice
1 teaspoon
hot pepper sauce
2 tablespoons vinegar
1 tablespoon canned
green chiles, minced
1 tablespoon
brown sugar
1 teaspoon cumin
1 bay leaf,
crushed

Rub lamb with olive oil, salt and pepper.
In a medium sauce pan, combine onions,
chili sauce, lemon juice, olive oil, hot pepper
sauce, vinegar, chiles, sugar, cumin and
crushed bay leaf and mix well. Cook
over medium heat for 20 minutes.
Place flattened lamb on a grill,
over medium-low coals.
Cook, turning
every 15 minutes,
for 2 hours. Baste lamb
with chile mixture every
10 to 15 minutes.
Serves 6.

✿ ✿ ✿ ✿ ✿

ENCHILADA CASSEROLE

A perennial favorite of both Norte-Americanos
and Mexicans, this Enchilada dish
is the perfect banquet food.

INGREDIENTS:

12 corn tortillas
3/4 cup oil
6 large green
onions, chopped
3 cups
enchilada sauce
3 cups Monterey
Jack cheese, shredded
1 can pitted ripe
olives, cut in quarters

Cut tortillas into quarters. Fry a few at a time in hot
oil for 30 seconds. Place on paper towels to absorb
excess oil. Preheat oven to 350°F. Set aside 1 tablespoon
green onion. Mix remaining green onions with cheese.
Spoon enchilada sauce evenly over the bottom of a
large casserole dish. Cover sauce with 1/3 of the tortillas.
Top with 1/3 of the sauce, making sure to cover all
tortillas in sauce. Top with 1/3 of the cheese mixture
and olives. Repeat layering ingredients. Bake for
20 minutes, or until cheese is melted. Garnish
with remaining green onions.
Serves 8.

A WORD ABOUT MEATS:

Enhance the natural flavors of meats by rubbing
with 2 cloves of halved garlic. Next, add 1 teaspoon of
dried sage with 1 teaspoon marjoram and 1 teaspoon
of salt. Sprinkle over meat and cook for added flavor.

CHILE FETTUCCINE

This pasta dish is unlike any other you may have
tasted. The smooth texture of the fettuccine and
the spicy taste of the sauce come together to
make this an unforgettable experience.

INGREDIENTS:

1 pound
package fettuccine
1 clove garlic,
minced
3/4 cup olive oil
3/4 cup fresh green
chiles, roasted,
peeled and sliced thin
1/2 cup red bell
pepper, sliced thin
1/2 cup piñon nuts
1 cup Parmesan
cheese, grated
Salt
Pepper

Cook fettuccine according to directions on package.
In a large skillet, sauté garlic, chiles, red pepper and
piñon nuts in olive oil. Mix with pasta and top with
Parmesan cheese and salt and pepper.
Serves 6.

A WORD ABOUT PASTA:

One ounce of pasta generally yields about 1/2 cup
of cooked pasta. This may vary depending
upon the type and shape of the pasta.

PORK TAMALE PIE

A hearty meal sure to satisfy even the biggest appetites.
Serve with a cool green salad to round out the meal.

INGREDIENTS FOR FILLING:

1 1/2 pounds ground pork
1/2 cup onion, chopped
2 cups cooked tomatoes
1 clove garlic
1 tablespoon chili powder
1 1/2 teaspoons salt
1/2 teaspoon oregano
1/4 teaspoon pepper

INGREDIENTS FOR CORNMEAL TOPPING:

1 cup yellow cornmeal
2 tablespoons flour
1 tablespoon sugar
2 tsp baking powder
1/2 teaspoon salt
1/2 cup milk
1 tablespoon oil
1 egg

To prepare filling, brown scrambled pork, stirring to
cook evenly. Purée onion, 1/2 of the tomatoes, garlic and
chili powder in a blender. Gradually add the remaining
tomatoes and blend until puréed. Pour tomato purée into
a skillet with meat. Bring to a boil. Simmer on low heat.
Stir in salt, oregano and pepper. Simmer covered for
30 minutes. To prepare cornmeal topping, mix cornmeal
with flour, sugar, baking powder and salt in a bowl.
Preheat oven to 425°F. Beat egg slightly. Beat in milk and
shortening. Add liquid ingredients to dry ingredients all at
once and stir lightly, just until all dry ingredients are
moistened. Do not beat. Spoon batter over simmering filling.
Bake 20 to 25 minutes, until topping is lightly browned.

CHILE RELLENO

There are many ways to stuff chiles, following
are two different types of Chile Rellenos, the standard
cheese filling and a flavorful combination of beef, pork,
almonds, and raisins. You will be pleased with both!

INGREDIENTS:

1/4 pound
Monterey Jack cheese
1 7 oz can whole green
chiles, seeded and kept whole
2 eggs, separated
Flour
Salt
Pepper

Cut cheese in 1/2 inch thick rectangles, 1 inch long.
Wrap cheese in chile and roll in flour that has been salt
and peppered to taste. For the batter; beat egg whites
until stiff and beat yolks lightly. Add yolks into whites and
fold in 2 tablespoons of flour. Gently drop the floured chiles
into the batter, one at a time. Place battered chiles on a
plate and slide into a pan of moderately hot oil. Fry until
golden brown, turning and basting to ensure even
cooking. Place on paper towels to drain excess oil.
Serves 4.

A WORD ABOUT MEXICAN MEALS:

In Mexico, the main meal of the day is generally served in
the middle of the day, sometime around 2 o'clock. A light
snack is usually eaten in the late afternoon or early
evening. Another snack, often just a dessert,
is usually served later in the evening.

FANCY CHILE RELLENOS

INGREDIENTS:

2 medium
onions, chopped
2 medium
tomatoes, chopped
1/8 teaspoon garlic powder
2 tablespoons oil
1/2 pound ground beef
1/2 pound ground pork
4 tablespoons sliced almonds
4 tablespoons raisins
8 whole canned
chiles, seeded
4 eggs
1/2 cup flour
Oil for frying
1 teaspoon salt
1/2 teaspoon pepper

Sauté onions in oil until tender. Add garlic powder
and ground meat and cook until brown, scrambling
meat while cooking. Add tomatoes, salt, pepper, almonds
and raisins. Cook on low. In a separate pan, beat
egg whites until stiff and add beaten egg yolks.
Stuff chiles with meat filling. Roll stuffed chiles in flour
and dip in egg batter. Heat 2 inches of oil in a deep skillet
and fry chiles until lightly browned, turning often. Place
on paper towels to absorb excess oils before serving.
Serves 8.

A WORD ABOUT AVOCADOS:

When avocados yield to gentle pressure they are ripe
and can be stored in a cool refrigerator for 4 or 5 days.

MARINATED BEEF ROAST

With just a little preparation time and overnight
marinating, a plain roast can become
a heavenly repast.

INGREDIENTS:

1 clove garlic,
minced
1 4 pound
beef roast, rolled
1 3/4 cups
dry red wine
1 tablespoon lime juice
3 tablespoons olive oil
2 tablespoons water
2 tablespoons flour
1 bay leaf
Salt
Pepper

Mix garlic, bay leaf, wine, lime juice, salt and pepper
in a large casserole dish. Place the roast in the
casserole dish and coat with mixture. Cover
dish and marinate in refrigerator overnight, turning
occasionally. Remove roast from dish and pat dry.
Preheat oven to 375°F. Heat oil in a skillet and brown
roast on all sides. Salt and pepper to taste and place
in a Dutch Oven. Pour marinade over roast and cover.
Cook for 2 hours. Uncover and bake for another
15 to 30 minutes. Remove meat and place on a
warm platter. Use drippings for gravy and
serve with rice and beans.
Serves 6.

GREEN MOLE AND PORK

INGREDIENTS:

1 1/2 pound
pork loin roast
3 cups water
5 romaine
lettuce leaves
1/4 cup parsley
2 tablespoons cilantro
1 small onion, chopped
1/4 cup hulled squash seeds
1 13 ounce can tomatillos
2 cloves
garlic minced
1 canned
whole green chile
1 tablespoon oil
1/4 teaspoon cumin

Trim fat from pork and cut pork loin into 1 inch
pieces. In a large saucepan place roast chunks, water,
1/2 onion, 1 clove garlic, salt and pepper to taste.
Bring to a boil, skimming foam from surface. Cover
and simmer on low for 1 hour. Toast squash seeds
in a small skillet until lightly browned, stirring often.
Grind cooled squash seeds in a blender and set aside.
Drain canned tomatillos and combine with chile, lettuce,
remaining onion, garlic, parsley and cilantro in a
blender. Blend until fine. Drain meat, reserving broth.
Return meat to pan. Heat oil in a skillet and sauté squash
seeds for 2 minutes. Add ground tomatillo mixture and
cook over low heat for 5 minutes. Add 1 cup strained
reserved broth and stir. Pour mixture over meat.
Add 1/2 teaspoon salt and cumin and simmer on low
for 20 to 30 minutes. Add more broth to taste.
Serves 4.

TAMALES

A traditional holiday favorite in many Mexican
homes, tamales are the perfect banquet food
for any occasion. Choose your favorite
filling from pages 92 to 95 to fill.

INGREDIENTS:

3 1/2 dozen
large dry corn husks
1 cup lard
4 cups masa harina
Beef or chicken stock
2 teaspoons salt
2 1/2 to 3 cups
warm meat filling
of your choice
(see pages 92 to 95)

Soak corn husks until soft and pliant
Beat lard until light and fluffy, using a mixer. Gradually
beat in masa harina and stock until dough sticks together and
has a paste-like consistency. Taste dough before adding salt.
If the stock is salty, you may not want to add more salt.
Dry corn husks by placing on a paper towel and patting dry.
Spread about 2 tablespoons tamale dough on center portion
of husk, leaving at least a 2 inch margin at both ends and
about 1/2 inch margin at right side. Spoon 1 1/2 tablespoons
filling onto dough. Wrap tamale, overlapping left side first,
then right side slightly over left. Fold bottom up and top down.
Lay tamales in top section of steamer with open flaps on
bottom. Tie with a string if husks are too short to stay closed.
Tamales may completely fill top section of steamer but
should be placed so there are spaces between them for
circulation of steam. Steam over simmering water for 1 hour,
or until corn husk can be peeled from dough easily.
Makes 3 1/2 dozen.

MEXICAN MEAT LOAF

Here we have another simple but fulfilling meal
that I have found to be very popular with everyone
I know, especially the younger people.

INGREDIENTS:

1 pound
ground beef
1/2 pound
ground pork
1/2 cup
onion, chopped
2/3 cup
uncooked oats
1 egg, beaten
1 cup
enchilada sauce
2 hard-boiled
eggs, cut in half lengthwise
1/4 cup pimento
stuffed green olives, sliced
1 teaspoon salt
1/4 teaspoon pepper

Preheat oven to 350°F. Combine ground beef, ground
pork, onion, oats, beaten egg, salt, pepper, and 1/2 cup
enchilada sauce, mixing well. Pack half of the meat
mixture into an average size loaf pan. Arrange hard boiled
eggs in a row down center of loaf. Arrange olive slices
on either side of eggs, gently press eggs and olives
into meat. Cover with remaining half of meat
mixture. Top with remaining sauce.
Bake for 1 hour.
Serves 4.

SABANA DE RES

Pound the tenderloin until very thin, like a bed sheet,
which is what "sabana" means in Spanish.

INGREDIENTS:

2 pounds
beef tenderloin
1 cup olive oil
1/2 onion, minced
1 teaspoon paprika
1/2 teaspoon cayenne pepper
1/2 cup minced green olives
2 cloves garlic, minced
1 teaspoon oregano, chopped
1 teaspoon basil, chopped
1/2 teaspoon cracked pepper

INGREDIENTS FOR SAUCE:

1/2 cup onion, julienned
1/2 poblano chile, julienned
2 cloves garlic, minced
1 tablespoon olive oil
2 cups heavy cream
1/2 cup Oaxaca cheese, shredded
4 tablespoons cilantro, chopped
Salt and pepper

Combine olive oil, onion, paprika, cayenne, olives,
garlic, oregano, basil and cracked pepper. Mix well and
set aside. Cut beef tenderloin into four steaks. Place
steaks between sheets of wax paper and pound each steak
with a meat mallet until steaks are only 1/8 inch thick.
Brush flattened meat, on one side only, with marinade and
let sit for a couple of hours. Sauté onion, poblano chile and
garlic in olive oil until tender. Add cream and reduce
until thickened. Remove pan from stove and add cheese,
cilantro and salt and pepper to taste. Cook meat, or
sabana, in a large, very hot skillet. Cook for about
a minute on each side. Roll steaks and cover with
sauce before serving.
Serves 4.

MEXICAN CHILE PIE

Another easy-to-make, great-to-eat meal.

INGREDIENTS:

6 corn tortillas
1 cup vegetable oil
1 onion, chopped
3 tomatoes, chopped
1 cup chicken, diced
3 poblano chiles,
skinned, seeded
and sliced in strips
1 cup cream
or half and half
1/2 cup Cheddar cheese,
shredded
1/2 teaspoon salt

Heat oil in a small pan and fry each tortilla until
firm but not crisp. Place on paper towels to
absorb excess oil. In a larger pan, heat 2 tablespoons
oil and cook onions and tomatoes for 20 minutes. Stir
in salt and set aside. Preheat oven to 400°F. Grease a pie
plate and make a bottom layer using 3 tortillas. Pour half
of the tomato mixture over the tortillas then layer with
diced chicken. Make another layer with the poblano
chiles and top that with 1/2 cup cream. Place half
of the cheese over cream and top with remaining
tortillas. Finish by layering remaining tomato
mixture, cream and cheese. Bake at 400°F
for 15 to 20 minutes. Let cool for
10 minutes before serving
in pie shaped pieces.
Serves 4 to 6.

CHILI SKILLET

INGREDIENTS:

1 pound ground beef
1 16 oz can tomatoes,
loosely cut and undrained
1 tablespoon flour
1/2 teaspoon chili powder
1/4 teaspoon salt
1 16 oz package frozen
seasoned mixed vegetables
1 cup Cheddar cheese, shredded

In a large skillet, cook beef until brown, drain. Combine
tomatoes, flour, chili powder and salt and mix well.
Mix frozen vegetables and tomato mixture into meat.
Bring to a boil. Cover and simmer on low heat for 8 minutes,
stirring often. Spread cheese over top and cover until
melted. Serve with warm tortillas and Spanish rice.
Serves 5.

RED PEPPER LAMB CHOPS

INGREDIENTS:

12 1/2" thick
lamb rib chops, trimmed
4 red bell peppers
2 tablespoons olive oil
Salt and pepper
Paprika

Prepare chiles, reserving juices and discarding seeds.
Cut peppers into strips. Place peppers in a pan and cover
with reserved juice. Add 1 tablespoon olive oil. Set aside.
Preheat broiler. Rub lamb with salt and pepper and paprika.
Brush with 1 teaspoon oil. Broil to desired doneness, about
6 minutes for medium. Pour pepper mixture over lamb
chops. Serve with ranch corn or other vegetable dish.
Serves 6.

PAELLA

Nothing can compare to this wonderful seafood
Paella! Serve with warm sourdough
bread for a satisfying meal.

INGREDIENTS:

1 cup rice
1/4 cup olive oil
2 patties chorizo
1 cup clam juice
1 cup chicken broth
1 cup peas
1/3 cup carrots, chopped
15 mussels, in shells
10 clams, in shells
10 raw shrimp,
in shells
(fresh or frozen)
Saffron

Pour oil and rice into a large skillet or Dutch Oven
and cook until rice becomes a golden brown.
Add chorizo, chicken broth, peas, carrots, clam juice
and a dash of saffron to rice. Mix well. Drop mussels,
clams and shrimp on top of rice and bring mixture to a boil.
Simmer, covered, for 20 minutes. Transfer to a
large bowl before serving.
Serves 8.

A WORD ABOUT SAFFRON:

Saffron, a native of the Mediterranean, is most often
used in Spanish, South American, and French dishes.
Saffron is the most expensive spice in the world
and is used more for color than for flavor. Saffron pieces
can be used in cooking but it is most often used ground.

FAJITAS

When the people in Texas first created this delectable dish they used marinated skirt steak. Many still do, however, I prefer using the more tender sirloin.

INGREDIENTS:

3 pounds
sirloin steak, trimmed
1/2 cup lime juice
3 tablespoons oil
3 cloves garlic,
minced
1 1/2 teaspoons
ground cumin
1 teaspoon oregano
4 small onions, sliced
3 bell peppers, sliced
15 flour tortillas
Salt and pepper
Sour Cream
Guacamole
Refried Beans
Salsa

Cut steak into 3 inch by 1 inch strips and place in a glass bowl. Add lime juice, oil, garlic, cumin, oregano, and salt and pepper to taste. Mix well, making sure to coat all beef. Add onion and bell pepper slices and cover. Refrigerate overnight or for at least 4 hours. Drain meat and vegetables. Heat oil in large skillet and sauté meat and vegetables until cooked to your liking. Serve with sour cream, guacamole, beans and salsa.
Serves 8.

CHICKEN TAMALE PIE

Once again the staple foods of the Southwest
are used to create another tasty meal.

INGREDIENTS FOR FILLING:

1/4 cup lard or cooking oil
1 cup onion, chopped
1 clove garlic, minced
1 16 ounce
can cooked tomatoes
1 1/2 teaspoons salt
1 tablespoon chili powder
1/2 teaspoon cumin
3 cups diced cooked chicken

INGREDIENTS FOR TAMALE DOUGH:

1/2 cup lard
3 cups masa harina
1 teaspoon baking powder
1/2 teaspoon salt
1 cup chicken stock

To prepare filling, heat lard in large pan. Add onion and
garlic and cook for 5 minutes, or until onion is tender.
Add tomatoes and seasonings. Bring tomatoes to a boil.
Mix well. Simmer on medium heat for 10 minutes.
Stir in chicken and simmer for 5 minutes. To prepare
tamale dough, beat lard until light and fluffy, using spoon
or mixer. Combine masa flour, baking powder and salt.
Gradually beat flour mixture and chicken stock into lard
until dough sticks together and has a paste-like consistency.
Preheat oven to 350°F. Grease a large casserole dish.
Press tamale dough onto bottom and sides of dish
in a 1/2 inch layer. Reserve dough to cover top.
Pour in prepared filling. Cover filling with
remaining dough and pat into a layer the
same thickness as the lining. Bake for 1 hour.
Serves 6.

TRIPE WITH CHILE

INGREDIENTS:

1 pound tripe
2 Tbsp bacon drippings
3 potatoes, peeled
and sliced very thin
1 onion, diced
1 clove garlic, minced
1/2 teaspoon salt
1 7 ounce can green chiles,
drained and chopped
2 tomatoes, sliced

Rinse tripe before placing in a pan, covering with water
and simmering for several hours. When tripe has been
cooked for at least 3 hours, drain and cut into 1/2 inch
strips. Preheat oven to 325°F. Heat bacon drippings in
a medium skillet and add sliced potatoes, onions, garlic,
salt, chiles and tripe, cooking until browned. Add
tomatoes. Cover and bake at 325°F for 35 minutes.

SHORT RIBS

INGREDIENTS:

4 pounds short ribs
1/3 cup mustard
1 tablespoon sugar
2 tablespoons lime juice
3 onions, chopped
2 cloves garlic, minced
1 teaspoon each salt and pepper

Combine mustard, sugar, lime juice, garlic, salt and
pepper. Spread over beef top with onions, and refrigerate
overnight in a glass dish, turning often. Heat oven to 350°F.
Remove ribs from marinade and cook in a Dutch oven on medium
heat until brown. Cover with onions and marinade
and bake for 1 1/2 hours, until beef is tender.
Serves 6.

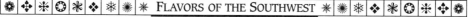

POULTRY
ROASTED, BARBECUED AND MORE

Poultry, the perfect meat for almost everyone,
is gaining popularity in kitchens around the world.
Here in the Southwest it is used more than any other
meat and has long been a favorite to generations of cooks,
from the earliest Native Americans and Mexicans to
newcomers from around the globe. A healthful alternative
to beef, chicken is often cooked skinless and served
without heavy sauces or gravies. Recipes offered
here are easily prepared, good for you,
and taste wonderful.

✸ ✸ ✸ ✸ ✸

LIME CHICKEN

Grill chicken with a selection of fresh vegetables for
a simply delicious meal

INGREDIENTS:

6 chicken breasts
3 limes
2 teaspoons basil,
chopped
4 tablespoons olive oil
2 teaspoons
white wine vinegar
Salt
Pepper

Remove skin from chicken. Salt and pepper
chicken and place in a baking dish. Using a citrus
zester, pare thin strips of rind from limes. Combine
lime juice, rind and wine vinegar with
4 tablespoons of olive oil. Pour mixture over chicken
and marinate for several hours. Preheat oven to
375°F. Baste chicken with lime mixture
and bake for 30 minutes.

✸ ✸ ✸ ✸ ✸

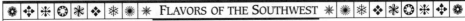

BLACKENED CHICKEN SALAD

The spices add a Cajun touch to this delightfully
spicy chicken dish. Serve with a glass of cool ice tea.

INGREDIENTS:

1 pound
boneless chicken breasts
1 bunch spinach
1 head romaine lettuce
1 cucumber, sliced
1 medium red onion,
thinly sliced
1/2 cup sunflower seeds
1 teaspoon garlic powder
1/2 teaspoon onion powder
1/2 teaspoon oregano
1/2 teaspoon
ground red pepper
1/2 teaspoon
black pepper
1/2 teaspoon salt
2 cups croutons
Salad dressing

Remove the skin from chicken. Combine garlic
powder, onion powder, oregano, red pepper, black
pepper and salt and rub all over chicken. Place
seasoned chicken on a broiler pan and place under
broiler for about 8 minutes, until chicken is cooked
thoroughly. Let chicken cool and cut into bite sized
pieces. Tear spinach and romaine lettuce into bite
sized pieces. In large salad bowl, combine spinach,
lettuce, onion rings, cucumber, croutons, sunflower
seeds with chicken pieces. Pour your favorite
dressing over the top and serve.
Serves 4.

❋ ❋ ❋ ❋ ❋

CHICKEN IN CHIPOTLE CHILE SAUCE

INGREDIENTS:

1/2 cup green chiles,
diced
1 4 pound chicken,
cut in pieces
1 16 ounce can
stewed tomatoes
5 canned chipotle chiles
1 small onion,
sliced thin
1/2 teaspoon
garlic powder
1 teaspoon oregano
1 1/2 teaspoons cumin
1/2 teaspoon cloves
1/4 teaspoon pepper
1 tablespoon chicken
bouillon granules
3 cups water
2 bay leaves
1 teaspoon salt

Combine green chiles, undrained tomatoes, chipotle chiles, garlic, oregano, cumin, clove and pepper. Place mixture in a blender and purée. Add bouillon granules. Set aside. In a large pot, place chicken, water, bay leaves and salt. Bring to a boil. Cover and simmer on low heat for 45 minutes. Drain broth. Add chipotle chile sauce and onion to chicken. Stir and coat chicken with sauce. Bring to a boil. Simmer on low heat for 20 minutes. Serve with a salad and corn on the cob. Serves 4.

✳ ✳ ✳ ✳ ✳

PEANUT CHICKEN

INGREDIENTS:

1 3 lb chicken fryer,
cut in pieces
5 cups water
1/8 teaspoon garlic powder
2 tablespoons mild chili powder
3 tablespoons peanut butter
2 tablespoons oil
1/3 cup sherry
Salt and pepper

Place chicken in a pot with 5 cups water. Add garlic and
salt. Cook until meat is tender and can be picked from bones.
Reserve broth and set aside. Combine chili powder, 2 1/2 cups
broth, peanut butter and sherry. Stir for 10 minutes, until sauce
is smooth. Add chicken to sauce and simmer for
10 minutes, until sauce thickens.
Serves 5.

✳ ✳ ✳ ✳ ✳

CHICKEN CHILE
CHEESE BURGERS

INGREDIENTS:

1 lb ground chicken
2 7 oz cans chiles, chopped
Salt and pepper
1/2 pound Monterey Jack
cheese slices
Hamburger Buns

Combine ground chicken, chopped chiles and salt and
pepper to taste. Form 4 good sized patties and grill
for about 20 minutes, or until done. Just before serving,
place a layer of chiles over burgers then top with a
slice of Jack cheese. Allow cheese to melt before serving.
Serves 4.

TURKEY AND MUSHROOM LOAF

A great way to utilize left over turkey, this tasty dish
should be served with a colorful selection of vegetables.

INGREDIENTS:

1 2 lb loaf of crusty bread
3 tablespoons melted butter
1 egg, beaten
2 cups cooked turkey,
shredded
1/2 pound mushrooms,
sliced
1 stalk celery, diced
6 tablespoons butter
1 onion, diced
1 1/2 tablespoons flour
1/2 teaspoon thyme
1/2 teaspoon tarragon
1/4 teaspoon nutmeg
1 tablespoon parsley,
chopped
Salt
Pepper

To prepare bread; preheat oven to 350ºF. Cut off the top
of the loaf of bread and remove soft bread inside. Melt
2 tablespoons butter and brush inside of the loaf
with butter. Brush with beaten egg. Bake for 8 minutes,
until bread is crispy and light brown. To prepare filling;
sauté onion and celery in 2 tablespoons butter until
tender. Stir in flour and remove pan from heat. Add chicken
stock, return to stove and bring to a boil, stirring often.
Simmer for 2 to 3 minutes. Remove from heat and
add turkey, thyme, tarragon and nutmeg and parsley.
Sauté mushrooms in remaining butter until tender.
Spread a layer of mushrooms in the bottom of the
loaf before adding turkey mixture. Top with
remaining mushrooms and replace lid. Bake for
5 to 10 minutes, until loaf becomes very hot.

❊ ❊ ❊ ❊ ❊

CHICKEN ENCHILADAS

INGREDIENTS:

3 cups cooked chicken, shredded
7 ounces green chili salsa, fresh or canned
1 4 ounce can chopped green chiles
2 1/2 cups heavy cream
1/2 cup Jack or Colby cheese
12 corn tortillas
1/2 teaspoon salt
1/2 head lettuce, shredded
12 olives

In a large bowl, combine cooked chicken, chiles and
salsa. In a shallow pan, mix cream and salt. Soften corn
tortillas by dipping into a pan of heated oil, then place
on paper towels to absorb extra oil. Dip each softened
tortilla into the cream mixture and fill with the chicken.
Roll filled tortillas and place in an ungreased baking dish.
Pour extra cream over enchiladas. Top with grated
cheese and bake, uncovered, for 25 minutes.
Garnish with shredded lettuce and olives. Serves 6.

✳ ✳ ✳ ✳ ✳

VERDE VALLEY TURKEY LOAF

INGREDIENTS:

1 1/2 pounds ground turkey
1 cup soft bread crumbs
1 cup canned, undrained tomatoes
3 tablespoons dried onion flakes
1 7 oz can green chiles, drained,
seeded and chopped
1 1/4 teaspoons salt
1/4 teaspoon garlic salt

Preheat oven to 375°F. Combine ground turkey, bread crumbs,
tomatoes, onion flakes, salt, chiles, and garlic salt. Mix well.
Place mixture in a large loaf pan and press lightly.
Bake for 45 minutes to 1 hour. Serves 6.

CHICKEN IN LEMON SAUCE

The lemon sauce gives this chicken dish a fresh flavor.
Serve with a side of Cilantro Rice to complete the feast.

INGREDIENTS:

4 chicken breasts
2 tablespoons olive oil
2 tablespoons butter
3 tablespoons flour
2 cups chicken broth
1 clove garlic
1 bay leaf
1/2 teaspoon oregano
2 egg yolks
3 tablespoons
fresh parsley, chopped
1 teaspoon lemon juice
4 slices of lemon
Salt and pepper

Season chicken with salt and pepper. In a skillet, heat
oil, butter and garlic and add chicken breasts. Fry
until golden brown, approximately 10 minutes. Remove
and set chicken aside. Drain off all but 2 tablespoons
of leftover oil. Add the flour to the oil and stir
for 1 minute. Add broth and bring to a boil, stirring
continuously. Return chicken to the pan. Add the bay
leaf and oregano and cover. Simmer for 30 minutes, until
tender. Remove chicken breasts from pan and place in a
warm serving dish. Remove herbs from sauce and discard.
Combine the egg yolks and lemon juice with 3 tablespoons
of the sauce and add to the pan, stirring continuously
until mixture thickens. Do not bring to a boil. Salt and
pepper to taste. Pour sauce over chicken and garnish
with lemon slices and fresh parsley.
Serves 4.

✳ ✳ ✳ ✳ ✳

CHICKEN AND RICE CASSEROLE

Words cannot describe the flavor of this wonderful dish.
And it tastes even better as a leftover.

INGREDIENTS:

2 whole chicken breasts
1/4 medium onion, chopped
1/8 teaspoon garlic powder
1 8.5 oz canned peas, drained
15 large Spanish green olive
1/2 teaspoon oregano
1 teaspoon salt
1/2 teaspoon pepper
1 tablespoon butter
1 cup uncooked long
grain rice, rinsed, drained
1 cup canned tomatoes,
undrained
6 peppercorns
1 quart water
Salt

Put chicken breasts in large pot. Add water,
garlic powder, onion, peppercorns and salt to taste.
Bring to a boil. Cover and simmer on low heat for
45 minutes, or until tender. Drain chicken and
reserve broth. Shred meat with fingers or by using
2 forks. Add olives, peas, oregano, 1 teaspoon
salt and pepper, let sit. Preheat oven to 350°F.
Heat butter in a large skillet. Add rice and sauté
until lightly browned. Pour tomatoes over rice and
press with a spoon. Let simmer for 5 minutes. Pour
into a 3 quart casserole dish and add chicken mixture.
Lightly mix. Strain 2 1/2 cups broth into mixture,
adding more if needed to cover mixture. Bake covered
for 1 hour. Let stand covered for 15 minutes before serving.
Serves 6.

✱ ✱ ✱ ✱ ✱

SPICED FRUITY CHICKEN

This is the perfect recipe to turn
to when plain chicken just won't do.
It is easy to prepare and
wonderful to eat.

INGREDIENTS:

2 frying chickens,
cut in pieces
1/2 cup crushed
pineapple
1 1/2 teaspoons salt
1/4 teaspoon pepper
1/4 teaspoon cinnamon
1/4 teaspoon
ground cloves
2 cloves garlic, minced
1/4 cup oil
1/2 cup onion,
chopped
1/2 cup raisins
2 cups orange juice
1/2 cup dry sherry

Combine salt, pepper, cinnamon, cloves, and garlic
and mix well. Rub into chicken. In a large skillet,
heat oil and brown chicken evenly. Place browned
chicken in a large pot. Saute onion in remaining oil
in skillet. Add onion to chicken along with raisins,
pineapple and orange juice. Add water, if needed,
to cover chicken. Bring to a boil. Cover and simmer
over medium heat for 1 hour, until chicken is
tender. Add sherry and cook for 5 more minutes.
Serves 8.

✳ ✳ ✳ ✳ ✳

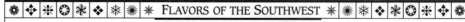

ROAST TURKEY

It's the jalapeño cornbread stuffing that
gives this traditional bird it's
Southwest flavor. A definite taste
treat for turkey lovers.

INGREDIENTS:

1 18 to 20 pound turkey,
thawed
Seasoned salt
Salt
Pepper

INGREDIENTS:

3 stalks celery, diced
1 onion, diced
5 jalapeño peppers,
cleaned,
seeded and diced
1/4 cup butter
2 loaves cornbread,
dried and crumbled
3 cups chicken stock

Remove giblets and neck and reserve for other uses.
Preheat oven to 325°F. Rinse and season turkey with
seasoning salt, salt and pepper. Sauté celery and
onion in butter until tender. In a medium mixing bowl,
combine sautéed celery and onion with the jalapeño
peppers, cornbread crumbs and 2 cups of chicken stock,
adding more stock if necessary. Stuff turkey and
place in a large roasting pan. Cook for approximately
5 hours, basting regularly. Turkey is done when leg
moves up and down freely and juice runs clear.
Serves 12.

✳ ✳ ✳ ✳ ✳

CHICKEN IN MUSHROOM SAUCE

Here is another wonderful selection for a dinner party.
Its first class taste will ensure your success of your event
and establish your reputation as an excellent cook.

INGREDIENTS:

2 frying chickens,
cut in serving pieces
1 16 oz can tomatoes,
undrained
1 lb fresh mushrooms,
cleaned and sliced
2 canned green
chiles, seeded
1/4 cup oil
1/2 cup onion,
chopped
1/4 teaspoon
garlic powder
1 cup chicken broth
1 cup sour cream
1 1/2 teaspoons salt

Brown chicken in hot oil in a large pan. Transfer to
a large pot. Sauté mushrooms in remaining oil in skillet.
Spoon over chicken. Set pan with oil to one side.
Combine tomatoes, chilies, onion, and garlic in a blender
and purée. Pour purée into remaining oil in skillet,
bring to a boil. Cook for 5 minutes, stirring in chicken
stock and salt. Pour sauce over chicken and mushrooms
in large pan. Cover and simmer on low for 1 hour, until
chicken is tender. Just before serving, add sour
cream and stir until heated through. Serve with rice.
Serves 8.

CHICKEN FAJITAS

Fajitas are a Texas creation that
have become popular all
across the Southwest.

INGREDIENTS:

2 pounds
boneless chicken breasts
1/2 cup lime juice
3 tablespoons oil
3 cloves garlic, minced
1 1/2 teaspoons
ground cumin
1 teaspoon oregano
4 small onions, sliced
3 bell peppers, sliced
15 flour tortillas
Salt and pepper
Sour Cream
Guacamole
Refried Beans
Salsa

Cut chicken into 3 inch by 1 inch strips and place
in a glass bowl. Add lime juice, oil, garlic, cumin,
oregano, and salt and pepper to taste. Mix well,
making sure to evenly coat chicken. Add onion
and bell pepper slices and cover.
Refrigerate overnight or for at least 4 hours.
Drain meat and vegetables. Heat oil in
large skillet and sauté meat and
vegetables until cooked.
Serve with sour cream,
guacamole, beans and salsa.
Serves 8.

✻ ✻ ✻ ✻ ✻

BARBECUED CHICKEN

This zesty sauce is quick to prepare and simply
tastes delicious. Why buy a sauce from the store
when you can whip one up at home?

INGREDIENTS:

1 can tomato purée
1/4 cup
canned pineapple juice
2 tablespoons vegetable oil
1 tablespoon fresh parsley,
chopped
1 tablespoon sugar
1 teaspoon salt
1/2 teaspoon chili powder
1/8 teaspoon hot pepper sauce
1/4 teaspoon pepper
1 3 lb broiler-fryer cut in pieces,
or 6 chicken breasts

Prepare grill. Mix tomato purée, pineapple juice, oil, salt,
parsley, sugar, hot pepper sauce, chili powder and
pepper. Cut chicken into serving pieces. Brush each
piece of chicken with tomato-pineapple sauce and place
chicken on grill over hot coals. Cook for 45 minutes to
1 hour, brushing on sauce and and turning often.
Serve with a rice dish and pineapple slices.
Serves 6.

❋ ❋ ❋ ❋ ❋

A WORD ABOUT SALSA:

Coat beef or chicken with salsa, using as a marinade,
before grilling or baking for more flavor. Or, serve fresh,
chunky salsa on the side to accommodate individual tastes.
Not only does this add flavor, but adds color to
the overall presentation.

❋ ❋ ❋ ❋ ❋

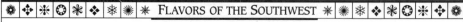
CHICKEN IN
SOUR CREAM SAUCE

A rich tasting chicken dish perfect for dinner parties.
Serve with green rice or Mexican rice.

INGREDIENTS:

1 5 pound roasting
chicken, pieced
1/4 cup
chicken broth
1/4 cup butter
1 medium onion,
chopped
1 clove garlic,
crushed
3 tablespoons butter
1/2 cup sour cream
1/2 cup heavy cream
2 cups flour
1 cup oil
1 1/2 tablespoon salt
1 1/2 tablespoon pepper

Cook chicken giblets and neck in pot of water to
make the broth. Combine flour, salt and pepper.
Coat chicken pieces with the seasoned flour and brown
in oil, turning to brown evenly. Grease a roasting
pan and arrange chicken in pan. Dot with butter and
pour broth over the chicken. Bake at 350°F until chicken
is tender, approximately 30 minutes. Sauté onion and
garlic in 2 tablespoons of butter and discard garlic.
Add sour cream, heavy cream and salt and pepper
to taste. Heat but do not boil. Place chicken on a
platter and pour sauce over chicken.
Serves 8.

✳ ✳ ✳ ✳ ✳

ROASTED CHICKEN
WITH ROSEMARY

Serve this elegant and savory dish with
Caramel Glazed Carrots and save the leftovers
for tasty Chicken Enchiladas.

INGREDIENTS:

3 2 to 2 1/2 pound
broiling chickens
4 to 5 sprigs
fresh rosemary
1/4 cup butter
1/2 cup white wine
1 cup chicken stock
1 cup heavy cream
1 teaspoon arrowroot
mixed with 1 tablespoon
water to form paste
Salt and pepper
Trussing needle and string

Preheat oven to 375°F. Place a sprig of rosemary
inside each chicken and truss them. In a large
baking or casserole dish, melt butter and brown
chickens on all sides. Place on one side and add wine,
half the stock and remaining rosemary leaves,
stripped from stems. Add salt and pepper and cover pan.
Bake for 30 to 40 minutes or until the chickens are tender.
Turn from side to side during cooking. Test by pricking
thigh, if no pink juice escapes, chickens are done.
Remove the trussing strings and place on a platter.
Keep warm. Add stock to cooking juices and
bring to a boil. Work juices and rosemary leaves
through a sieve to purée. Return sauce to pan and add
cream. Bring just to a boil and add arrowroot paste until
sauce thickens slightly. Taste for seasoning before
spooning sauce around chickens, or serve on the side.
Serves 6.

✳ ✳ ✳ ✳ ✳

SEAFOOD
FROM CEVICHE TO SALMON

Seafood has always been a large part of Mexican
cooking due to Mexico's abundant coastline. The easy
availability of fresh fish throughout most of the Southwest
means you can make a fish taco almost as easily as a
beef taco, or you can prepare a spicy *Snappy Red Snapper*
or the smooth essence of *Cold Lobster with Apricot Sauce*
with a simple visit to your local market. Grilling fish on the
barbeque almost year round is a definite advantage of
Southwest living. A topping of flavorful salsa adds an
exciting touch of Southwestern flavor to any fish.

SHRIMP AND SCALLOP CEVICHE

INGREDIENTS:

1/2 pound shrimp, shelled,
deveined and diced
1/2 pound scallops, diced
1 cucumber,
peeled and diced
1 carrot, diced
1 scallion, diced
1/4 cup fresh cilantro,
chopped
1/4 teaspoon
crushed red pepper
Lemon juice
Salt and pepper

Place diced scallops and shrimp in a bowl and rinse well.
Add lemon juice to cover and refrigerate for
2 1/2 to 3 1/2 hours. In a medium mixing bowl combine
cucumber, carrot, scallion, cilantro and red pepper. When
shrimp and scallops have become opaque, remove from
lemon juice and add to the bowl of vegetables.
Add the juice of one fresh lemon and salt and pepper to taste.
Serves 6.

WHITE FISH
WITH AVOCADO SAUCE

Avocados give this white fish a creamy, savory
flavor that everyone at your table will relish.

INGREDIENTS:

1 1/2 pounds white fish
fillets, fresh or frozen
5 peppercorns
1/4 teaspoon salt
1 bay leaf, crushed
3 or 4 onion slices
Juice of 1/2 lemon
Water

INGREDIENTS FOR AVOCADO SAUCE:

1 large ripe avocado,
peeled and sliced
1/2 teaspoon
Worcestershire sauce
1/2 cup whipping cream
1 teaspoon lemon juice
1/2 cup milk
4 parsley sprigs
1/2 teaspoon
white pepper
1/2 teaspoon salt

To prepare avocado sauce; place avocado slices,
whipping cream, milk, lemon juice, salt, pepper,
Worcestershire sauce and parsley in blender and blend
until smooth. Cook over medium heat in a saucepan,
stirring often, do not bring to a boil. Set aside. Keep
warm. To prepare fish; place fish in large skillet and
add water to cover. Add peppercorns, bay leaf, salt,
onion slices and lemon juice. Bring to a boil. Cover
and simmer on low heat for 10 minutes or until
fish flakes easily when tested. Drain fish and place
on a warm plate. Pour sauce over fish and
garnish with parsley. Serve hot.

PASTA WITH MUSSELS

This delightful pasta dish with its creamy
sauce is a wonderful meal to
serve when entertaining.

INGREDIENTS:

10 pounds mussels
2 1/2 cups
dry white wine
5 shallots, diced
1 bay leaf
1 1/2 teaspoons pepper
3 cups heavy cream
1/2 cup parsley,
chopped fine
1/4 cup dry sherry
1 pound linguine
1 teaspoon salt

Rinse mussels thoroughly, discarding any that are
already open and making sure to remove the beards.
Add wine, shallots, bay leaf and pepper in a large pot.
Bring to a boil and add mussels. Cover pot and steam
on high heat until they open, about 2 minutes. Remove
pot from heat and set aside. When mussels are cool,
pour liquid into a bowl. Remove mussel shells. Strain
mussel fluid through several layers of cheesecloth
into pan. Bring fluid to a boil and reduce it down to
1/2 cup. Skim if necessary. Add cream, stirring
constantly, and let it boil down to half the volume.
Add 1/4 cup parsley and salt. Add sherry and shelled
mussels. Cover and cook over extremely low heat.
Prepare pasta as directed on package. Drain and
transfer to large serving bowl. Add sauce and
mix gently. Garnish with remaining parsley.
Serves 6.

WHITE FISH TACOS

Fish tacos have gained popularity at many
Mexican restaurants and taco stands in the Southwest.

INGREDIENTS:

1 pound white fish fillets
1 medium tomato,
chopped fine
1/4 cup scallions,
chopped fine
2 tablespoons canned
green chiles
2 tablespoons lemon juice
1 cup hot cooked spinach,
chopped
8 taco shells
1 cup sour cream
Salt
Pepper

Poach fish with lemon juice and water to cover until
fish is opaque and flakes easily with a fork.
Combine tomatoes, scallions, salt and chiles in a bowl.
Drain fish and cut into small chunks, removing any
bones or skin. Place equal amounts of fish on each taco
shell, add hot spinach and top with tomato sauce.
Garnish with sour cream and serve.
Serves 8.

A WORD ABOUT FISH:

Fish cooks very rapidly so be sure not to over cook.
Constant supervision of grilled fish is necessary.
Fish is cooked completely when translucent
flesh turns opaque and flaky.

BAKED RED SNAPPER

Even if fish is not your favorite food, you won't be able
to resist this dish. Serve with a simple rice dish
to complete the meal.

INGREDIENTS:

2 pounds
red snapper fillets
1 medium onion, sliced
2 tablespoons olive oil
5 medium
tomatoes, chopped
1/8 teaspoon
garlic powder
1 teaspoon oregano
2 tablespoons capers
1/4 cup white wine
1/2 cup black olives,
pitted
1 teaspoon cumin
Juice from 1 lemon
1 cup milk
Salt
Pepper

Cut fish into 8 pieces and place in a casserole dish.
Mix oregano in milk and pour over fish. Refrigerate
for 2 hours, covered. In a large skillet, sauté onion in oil.
Add tomatoes, garlic powder, capers, wine, cumin, lemon
juice and olives. Simmer for 15 minutes or until thickened.
Drain fish and dry with paper towels. Make 8 sturdy aluminum
foil squares, 12 inches wide. Place a fish fillet on each foil
square. Spoon equal amounts of vegetable mixture over
each piece of fish. Fold foil until securely sealed. Put
foil packs on a baking sheet and cook at 350°F for
30 minutes. Fish is done when it flakes easily with
a fork. Garnish with cilantro.
Serves 8.

AHI TUNA
WITH PAPAYA SALSA

What a treat this is! There is nothing like this
delectable combination for a dinner party.

INGREDIENTS:

6 7 ounce Ahi steaks

INGREDIENTS FOR SALSA:

2 papayas, peeled,
seeded and chopped
1 small
red onion, diced
1 serrano chile,
seeded and diced
1 small red bell pepper,
seeded and diced
1 tablespoon water
2 tablespoons peanut oil
1/2 cup fresh mint leaves
1/2 cup lime juice
Salt
Pepper

To prepare salsa; in a medium pan, combine onion,
chile, bell pepper, water and oil. Simmer over low heat
for 10 minutes. Remove to medium mixing bowl.
Blanch mint leaves by dipping in boiling water for one
minute. Cool in ice water and dry with paper towels.
Dice mint leaves and add to vegetable mixture. Add
papayas, lime juice, salt and pepper to taste. Set
aside to marinate for 1 hour. To prepare steaks;
grill steaks on a hot grill for 2 to 3 minutes
per side. Top with salsa and serve.
Serves 6.

LOBSTER WITH APRICOT SAUCE

This lobster dish, served cold, is my version of a
recipe I tasted in London several years ago.

INGREDIENTS:

4 1 to 2 pound lobsters
4 apricots, halved
Sprig of mint

INGREDIENTS FOR SAUCE:

1/2 cup onion, diced
1 tablespoon oil
1 1/2 teaspoons curry powder
3/4 cup red wine
1 bay leaf
1 teaspoon tomato paste
1 tablespoon lemon juice
1 1/2 cups mayonnaise
2 1/2 tablespoons apricot preserves
2 tablespoons heavy cream
Dash of Tabasco sauce

To prepare lobster; using a large pot, place a rack inside
pot to sit 2 to 3 inches above the bottom. Add water
to just below rack. Cover and bring water to a boil. When
steam begins to escape from pot, add lobsters. Cover
and begin timing. When steam begins to escape from lid,
cook 12 to 14 minutes. Remove lobsters and chill for
30 minutes. Remove meat from lobster tail and claws and
set aside. To prepare sauce; sauté onion in oil in a medium
pan until onion becomes light brown. Add curry powder
and cook for 1 minute. Add wine, bay leaf, tomato paste,
lemon juice and Tabasco. On high heat, reduce mixture until
3/4 cup remains. Remove bay leaf and discard. Pour mixture
into smaller bowl and chill for 5 minutes. Combine mayonnaise,
wine and onion mixture and apricot preserves and purée in a
food processor or blender until smooth. Add salt to taste. Slice
meat from lobster tails down center, opening wide. Spoon sauce
over middle of lobster tail and around meat. Arrange claw-meat
on side, on top of sauce and serve.
Garnish with apricot halves and mint.

WHITE FISH IN TOMATILLO SAUCE

Tomatillos are a small tomato-like vegetable
with an outer papery husk, if they are unavailable,
use green tomatoes.

INGREDIENTS:

1 1/2 pounds white fish fillets
3 tablespoons lime juice
3 tablespoons oil
1/2 teaspoon salt

INGREDIENTS FOR SAUCE:

1 pound tomatillos
3 green onions, chopped
1 clove garlic
1 tablespoon parsley
1 mild green
pepper, cleaned and seeded
2 teaspoons oil
Salt

Remove husks from tomatillos and wash well. In a
medium saucepan, pour 1/2 inch water and add fresh
tomatillos. Bring to a boil then cover, reduce heat,
and cook until tomatillos become tender, about
10 minutes. Drain and cool. Place tomatillos,
green onions, garlic, parsley and chile in a food
processor or blender and purée. In a medium saucepan,
heat 2 teaspoons oil and add purée. Salt to taste and
bring to a boil. Simmer over reduced heat, uncovered, for
15 minutes. Prepare fish by sprinkling with lime juice
and salt. Let stand for 45 minutes. In a large skillet,
heat 3 tablespoons oil and cook fish for 1 minute on
each side. Add sauce and cover. Simmer for
5 minutes or until fish becomes flaky.
Serves 6.

HOLIDAY CODFISH

INGREDIENTS:

1 pound salted codfish
5 pickled chiles,
seeded and cut in strips
2 small onions, peeled
3 medium tomatoes,
peeled, seeded and chopped
3 canned pimentos,
cut in strips
1/2 cup pimento-stuffed olives
1 tablespoon chopped parsley
2 cloves garlic, peeled

Soak codfish for 3 hours in cold water, changing
water often. Drain and put in saucepan, covering
with water. Add 1 onion, and simmer, covered,
until fish flakes easily when tested with fork. Drain.
Salt and pepper to taste. Puree tomatoes, 1 onion and
garlic in a blender. Add oil to sauce and cook in
a skillet, stirring often. Mix in chile and pimento strips.
Place codfish on a plate and cover with sauce.
Garnish with olives and parsley.

A WORD ABOUT SHELLFISH:

Live oysters, mussels, clams and scallops should
have tightly closed shells. Shells should not be cracked,
chipped or broken in any way. If shells are open,
tap the shell to discover if fish are alive. Live shellfish
will close up tight if disturbed. Do not cook dead,
unshucked clams, mussels, oysters or scallops. Shucked
clams, mussels and oysters should be plump and
surrounded by clear, opalescent liquid. Fresh shellfish
should have a mild odor.

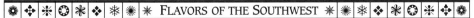

SALMON IN SHALLOT SAUCE

The combinations of flavors and textures give this
savory salmon dish an elegant appeal. Serve
with your favorite white wine.

INGREDIENTS FOR SALMON:

5 pounds salmon
2 cups white wine
1 cup water
2 bay leaves
2 small onions
8 peppercorns

INGREDIENTS FOR SHALLOT SAUCE:

1/2 cup dry white wine
1 teaspoon shallots, diced
2 cups heavy cream
1/2 teaspoon salt
1/2 teaspoon white pepper
1 cup capers

To prepare shallot sauce; place wine and shallots in
a saucepan and bring to a boil over medium heat.
Cook until mixture has reduced to 1/2, about
5 minutes. Add cream and salt and white pepper and
cook over low heat, stirring often with a wire whisk.
Cook until mixture reduces to 1 1/2 cups and strain
through a sieve. Set aside. To prepare salmon; add
wine, water, bay leaves, onions and peppercorns to
the bottom of a fish poacher and bring to a boil. Wrap
salmon in cheesecloth or place on a rack in poacher
before placing in the water. Lower heat and cook for
10 to 15 minutes. When inserted knife comes out
clean, fish is done. Place salmon on individual
serving plates and spoon shallot sauce over most of the
fish and onto the plate. Garnish lavishly with capers.
Serves 6.

VERACRUZ SHRIMP

Here is another excellent recipe featuring
shrimp, prepared Veracruz style.

INGREDIENTS:

1 pound fresh medium
shrimp, peeled, and
deveined
12 pimento
stuffed green olives
5 small tomatoes,
chopped and peeled
1 large green pepper
1 small onion, chopped
1 1/2 teaspoons capers
1/2 teaspoon sugar
1/2 teaspoon salt
1/2 teaspoon pepper
2 tablespoons oil
1 tablespoon oil
Lemon juice

Cut green pepper into 1 inch pieces.
Sauté onion and green pepper. Add
tomatoes, capers, olives, sugar and salt.
Bring mixture to boil. Cover and simmer
on medium low heat for 20 minutes.
Taste sauce and add salt to taste.
In a large skillet, heat 2 tablespoons
of oil and add shrimp. Cook over
medium heat until pink,
approximately 2 minutes.
Sprinkle lemon juice over shrimp
and add sauce. Let simmer over
low heat for 3 to 4 more minutes.
Serve hot. Serves 4.

SWORDFISH KABOBS

An incredibly savory barbecued meal, serve with cornbread and a selection of side dishes.

INGREDIENTS:

1 pound swordfish fillets
1/4 cup lime juice
1/4 cup vegetable oil
1 tablespoon cilantro,
chopped
1/2 teaspoon salt
1 clove garlic,
minced
1/2 jalapeño,
seeded and chopped
1 cup pineapple chunks
2 zucchini,
cut into 1/2 inch slices
1 red bell pepper,
cut in squares

Cut fish into 3/4 inch chunks. Combine lime juice, oil, cilantro, salt, garlic and jalapeño pepper in a glass bowl. Mix well and add fish chunks. Cover and refrigerate for at least 2 hours, turning often. Remove fish and reserve marinade. Alternately thread fish, pineapple, zucchini and bell pepper on 11 inch skewers, leaving a little room between each piece. Place full skewers over a heated grill, or on a rack in a broiler pan. Brush with marinade, turning and brushing often for about 5 minutes, or until fish becomes flaky. Serve with rice or a side of beans. Serves 4.

MEXICAN FRIED FISH

Once again, we take what is often an ordinary dish
and turn it into something really special.

INGREDIENTS:

1 pound fish fillets,
fresh or frozen
2 tablespoons lime juice
1/2 cup flour
1/4 cup oil
Salt
Pepper

INGREDIENTS FOR SAUCE:

2 tablespoons olive oil
1 small onion, chopped
1/2 cup green pepper,
chopped
1/2 cup celery,
chopped
1/2 teaspoon garlic powder
2 tablespoons dry sherry
1 cup canned peeled tomatoes,
drained and chopped
Salt and pepper
Saffron

Sprinkle fish with lime juice, salt and pepper and
let sit. Heat olive oil and add green pepper, celery,
onion, and garlic. Sauté until tender. Add sherry,
tomatoes and salt and pepper to taste. Add a dash
of saffron. Simmer, stirring occasionally. Drain fish
and coat with flour. Heat oil and fry fish until lightly
brown, turning once. Drain fish and place on paper
towel to absorb excess oils. Serve on warm
plates, topping with sauce.
Serves 4.

WHITE FISH IN BLACK SAUCE

The seasonings, along with the raisins, beer and wine,
come together to create this mouth watering delight.

INGREDIENTS:

1 1/2 pounds
white fish fillets
2 tablespoons butter
2 carrots, diced
2 stalks of celery, diced
1 medium onion,
chopped fine
1 bay leaf
1/2 teaspoon
dried thyme
2 sprigs parsley
1/2 teaspoon salt
1/2 teaspoon pepper
1 1/2 cups dark beer
1 cup red wine
3 tablespoons lemon juice
2 teaspoons sugar
1/4 cup chopped walnuts
1/4 cup seedless raisins
2 tablespoons plum jam
1/4 cup blanched
almonds, chopped

Sauté carrots, celery and onion in butter until tender,
about 5 minutes. Add bay leaf, thyme, parsley, salt
and pepper. Add 1 cup beer, wine, lemon juice, sugar,
walnuts, raisins and jam. Stir to mix and cook for 15 minutes.
If the sauce becomes too thick, add more beer. Place fish
in a skillet and spoon sauce over top. Poach over medium heat
for about 15 minutes, until fish is done. Place fish fillets on
individual plates and spoon sauce over top, discarding
bay leaf. Garnish with almonds.
Serves 4.

SNAPPY RED SNAPPER

INGREDIENTS:

1 lb red snapper fillets,
cut into 1/4 inch strips
1/2 cup onion, sliced
1/2 cup celery, sliced
1/2 cup bell pepper, sliced
2 fresh jalapeño peppers, sliced
1 clove garlic, minced
3 tablespoons olive oil

Heat olive oil in a large skillet and add onion,
celery, bell pepper, jalapeño pepper and garlic. Sauté
for 4 minutes before adding strips of fish. Turn fish
strips until evenly cooked and serve,
spooning vegetables over top.
Serves 4.

TARTAR SAUCE

INGREDIENTS:

3/4 cup mayonnaise
3 tablespoons pickle, minced
2 teaspoons onion flakes
1 tablespoon lemon juice
1/4 teaspoon dry mustard
1/4 teaspoon celery salt
1 teaspoon capers, minced

Combine mayonnaise, pickle, onion flakes, lemon juice,
mustard, celery salt and minced capers. Mix well
and refrigerate for several hours. Serve with your
favorite baked, fried or grilled fish.
Makes 1 cup.

RICH SHRIMP

Rich is the only word I can find to
describe this wonderful creation, which
can also be served as an appetizer.

INGREDIENTS:

1 lb shrimp,
peeled and deveined
1 5 oz can
evaporated milk
2 tablespoons butter
1 slice bacon,
chopped
2 ounces Swiss
cheese, shredded
2 tablespoons
dairy sour cream
1 tablespoon parsley,
minced
1/2 teaspoon
Worcestershire sauce
1/2 cup white wine
Salt
White pepper
Steamed white rice

Mix butter and bacon in a large non-stick pan. Over
medium heat, cook until bacon is lightly browned.
Add shrimp and cook until pink, stirring for about
2 minutes. Place cooked shrimp on a warm plate,
leaving juices in pan. Add wine to pan and cook
until mixture is reduced to 1/3 cup. Add milk and
simmer for 1 minute, stirring constantly. Add
Worcestershire sauce, salt and pepper to taste. Add
cheese gradually, stirring until melted. Return
shrimp to pan. Cook on low for 2 minutes, stirring
constantly. Stir in sour cream and blend well. Do not boil.
Serve over steamed white rice and garnish with parsley.
Serves 4.

FISH CAMPECHE STYLE

Serve this incredible dish to someone who
doesn't like fish and create a friend for life.
Serve with black beans as a side dish.

INGREDIENTS:

1 pound fish fillets,
fresh or frozen
1 cup orange juice
1 6 ounce
can tomato paste
1 cup water
1/4 cup onion,
chopped
1 teaspoon chili
powder
Salt
Pepper

Place fish in a medium pan and add water to cover.
Add 1/2 cup of orange juice. Bring to a boil. Simmer
on low for 10 minutes, or until fish flakes when
tested with a fork. Drain and skim, if necessary.
Cut fish into finger-sized pieces. Return to pan. In
a separate saucepan, combine remaining orange juice,
tomato paste, 1 cup of water, onion, and chili powder.
Bring to a boil. Season with salt and pepper to taste.
Pour sauce over fish and simmer until sauce thickens.
Serves 6.

A WORD ABOUT CENTERPIECES:

A creative centerpiece can add fun, flair and beauty
to any table setting. A simple straw cowboy hat,
resting upside down, can be filled with fresh
flowers for a lovely Southwestern centerpiece.

ORANGE FISH

Here is a sinfully delicious creation that is
also really good for you. Garnish
with thin orange slices.

INGREDIENTS:

4 fish fillets
1/4 cup lime juice
4 tablespoons olive oil
3 scallions,
chopped fine
1/8 teaspoon garlic powder
1 large tomato,
peeled, seeded and diced
1/2 cup orange juice
2 tablespoons
capers, drained
2 tablespoons dry sherry

Place fish fillets in a baking dish and sprinkle
with salt, pepper and lime juice. Let stand for 1/2 hour.
Preheat oven to 350°F. Using a tablespoon of olive oil,
lightly grease a shallow baking dish. Place fish,
salt and pepper side down in baking dish. In a
small bowl, mix scallions, tomato, garlic,
remaining olive oil, and capers. Spread mixture
over fish. Bake for 10 minutes before pouring
orange juice and sherry over fish. Bake for
another 10 minutes, until fish is done.
Serves 4.

A WORD ABOUT SUBSTITUTIONS:

Remember, you can always substitute your favorite
fish or seafood when preparing recipes in this
and all the other chapters.

SIDE DISHES
ANASAZI BEANS TO SEDONA RICE

Beans and rice are staples of the Mexican diet
and are very important to the Southwesterner as
well. Vegetables, such as squash, corn, zucchini,
potatoes, carrots and the ever present chile, are also
very important ingredients in Southwestern cooking.
Traditional dishes like *Refried Beans* and *Sedona Rice*
are joined in this section with *Greens with Chiles*
and my *Western Potato Wedgies* to help
round out your next meal.

MEXICAN SUCCOTASH

My good friend Cathy is a vegetarian who loves Succotash.
This is a Mexican variation of her own recipe.

INGREDIENTS:

3 medium zucchini,
sliced
1 medium onion,
chopped
1 green pepper,
seeded and diced
1/4 cup canned pimiento,
diced
2 large tomatoes, peeled,
seeded and chopped
1 1/2 cups corn,
fresh or frozen
1/4 cup butter
Salt and pepper

In a large skillet sauté onion in butter until tender. Add
zucchini, onion, green pepper, pimiento, tomatoes and corn.
If mixture is too dry, add 1/2 cup water or chicken broth.
Add salt and pepper to taste and simmer until
vegetables are tender.
Serves 6.

STUFFED ARTICHOKES

INGREDIENTS:

4 artichokes
1/4 cup white wine
1 1/2 cups vegetable stock
1 tablespoon butter
1/2 tablespoon flour
3/4 pound mushrooms
3 tablespoons butter
1 medium onion, diced
1 medium carrot, diced
1/2 cup chopped ham
2 tablespoons parsley, chopped
1 teaspoon oregano
1 teaspoon marjoram
1/2 cup fresh breadcrumbs
Salt and pepper

To prepare artichokes; trim stalks of artichokes and, using scissors, trim leaves and tops to remove spines. Wash artichokes thoroughly and place in salted water. Bring to a boil. Boil for 35 to 45 minutes, until a leaf can be pulled away with little effort. Drain, rinse and cool. To prepare filling; chop mushrooms, reserving 4 large mushrooms. Sauté onion and carrot, in 1 tablespoon butter, until soft. Add chopped mushrooms and cook for 4 or 5 minutes, until all moisture has evaporated. Remove pan from heat and add ham, parsley, oregano, marjoram and enough breadcrumbs to make a firm mixture. Add salt and pepper to taste. Remove center leaves from artichokes and scoop out hairy chokes. To finish; preheat oven to 350°F. Fill center with mushroom mixture, topping with whole mushroom and pat of butter. Tie a string around artichokes to hold leaves in place and arrange artichokes in a deep baking dish. Pour wine and stock around artichokes and cover baking dish with lid or foil. Bake for 35 to 40 minutes, until tender. Place artichokes on a serving platter and keep warm. Mix butter and flour together and set aside. Strain cooking fluid before reheating. Whisk butter and flour mixture into cooking liquid to thicken. Simmer for 2 minutes and add salt and pepper to taste. Pour sauce around baked artichokes and serve. Serves 4.

REFRIED BEANS

Beans are the most commonly eaten food in
the Mexican diet and are served at every meal.

INGREDIENTS:

1 pound red beans
1 1/2 quarts water
1 cup lard or bacon drippings
Salt

Soak beans overnight. Add more water to cover and add
salt. Cook on very low heat until beans become tender.
Mash the beans before adding 1/2 cup very hot bacon
drippings or lard. Continue cooking until the fat has been
absorbed, stirring often to avoid sticking. Heat additional
fat in a frying pan and add beans. Cook and stir
until beans become dry.

ANASAZI BEANS

INGREDIENTS:

2 cups Anasazi beans
4 cups water
1/4 cup oil
1 onion, chopped
1 clove garlic, minced
1/2 green bell pepper, chopped
1/2 red bell pepper, chopped
1 teaspoon chili powder
1 teaspoon salt

Sort and rinse beans. Place beans in water and cover.
Soak overnight. Bring water to a boil. Simmer for one hour.
Drain and reserve 1 cup liquid. Sauté onion and garlic in oil
for 5 minutes. Add bean fluid and bell peppers, chili powder
and salt. Cook on low heat for 45 minutes, stirring often.
Add beans and simmer for 15 minutes. Serve hot or cold.
Serves 6.

WESTERN POTATO WEDGIES

I first tasted this dish while visiting my friend Mary in
Knoxville, Tennessee. I have adapted it to my own taste
and have prepared it for friends and family who now
refer to them as "Dorothy's Potatoes."

INGREDIENTS:

6 medium potatoes
1/4 cup butter
1/4 cup oregano, chopped
1/4 cup parsley, chopped
1 small onion, chopped
Salt
Pepper

Preheat oven to 375°F. Scrub potatoes and slice into wedges.
Melt butter. Put potato wedges and chopped onion in a baking
dish and pour butter over the top, coating evenly. Sprinkle
oregano, parsley, salt and pepper to taste over potatoes and
bake for 45 minutes or until desired crispness is reached.
Use a slotted spoon to occasionally turn the potatoes.
Serves 5.

CHILI BEANS

INGREDIENTS:

1/2 pound pinto beans
4 1/2 cups water
1 teaspoon salt
1 teaspoon chili powder
1 medium onion, chopped
1/4 teaspoon crushed red pepper

Rinse beans, removing any foreign objects. Add water,
bring to a boil. Cover and cook for 3 minutes. Cover and set
aside to soak for 1 hour. Add salt, chili powder, red pepper
and onion. Bring to a boil. Cover and simmer for 1 to 2 hours
on low heat until beans are tender, stirring often.
Serves 4.

SEDONA RICE

This rice dish has all the beautiful colors of Sedona.
Excellent when served with grilled chicken.

INGREDIENTS:

2 tablespoons butter
1 clove garlic, minced
1 large onion, chopped
1 1/4 cups uncooked rice
1 16 ounce can tomatoes
1 13 oz can chicken broth
Salt and pepper

In a medium sauce pan, sauté onion and garlic in butter
until tender. Add rice, tomatoes, chicken broth, salt and pepper
to taste. Bring to a boil and cover. Simmer for 15 minutes,
until all the liquid is absorbed and the rice is tender.
Serves 6.

POTATO BALLS

INGREDIENTS:

3 medium baked potatoes
1/2 cup water
3 tablespoons butter
2 eggs
1/2 cup flour
Oil for frying
Salt and pepper

While potatoes are hot, scrape out insides and mash smooth.
Measure 2 cups of potatoes and place in a pan. Add boiling water,
butter and flour all at once. Mix well until mixture separates
from side of the pan. Add eggs, unbeaten, one at a time and beat
well. Add salt and pepper to taste. Shape into balls and
deep fry in hot oil until lightly brown.
Makes 20 balls.

RANCH CORN

This is an easy to make corn dish that goes
great with grilled chile burgers, or hot dogs.

INGREDIENTS:

6 slices bacon, diced
2 tablespoons onion,
chopped
1 4 1/2 oz can of mushrooms,
drained
2 12 oz cans whole-kernel corn with
peppers, drained
3/4 cup Monterey Jack cheese,
shredded

Fry bacon until cooked but not brown. Drain excess fat
and add mushrooms and onion and sauté. Add corn and cook
thoroughly. Sprinkle with grated cheese and heat until
cheese melts. Do not stir.
Serves 6.

SPANISH VERMICELLI

INGREDIENTS:

1 package vermicelli
3 tablespoons oil
2 cups chicken broth, or water
1 onion, diced
2 tomatoes, peeled and chopped
1/2 cup grated cheese
1 teaspoon salt and pepper

Lightly brown the vermicelli in the oil, breaking if
necessary, and set aside. Combine onion, tomato, broth,
salt and pepper in a medium pot. Bring to a boil and
add vermicelli. Cover and simmer over low heat
until all liquid has been cooked. Garnish with cheese.
Serves 4.

STUFFED AVOCADOS

On hot summer days these stuffed avocados make a
cool, elegant meal. Serve with a bowl of Gazpacho
soup and a glass of Sangria or Sun Tea.

INGREDIENTS:

2 large avocados
2 tablespoons lemon juice
2 tomatoes, peeled,
seeded and diced
4 scallions, diced
1/2 teaspoon basil
4 green olives, chopped
4 tablespoons olive oil
1 1/2 tablespoons vinegar
1 teaspoon sugar
4 tablespoons mayonnaise
Cayenne pepper
1/2 head of lettuce
Salt and pepper

Peel avocados and cut in half, lengthwise. Remove the pits
and brush avocados with lemon juice to prevent browning.
Combine oil, basil, vinegar, sugar, salt and pepper to taste
and a pinch of cayenne pepper, mixing well. Add tomatoes,
scallions, and olives to the oil mixture and add mayonnaise,
blending well. Fill avocados with mixture and serve on a bed
of lettuce. Garnish with a pinch of Cayenne pepper.
Serves 4.

A WORD ABOUT BAY LEAVES

Bay leaves come from evergreen trees in the Mediterranean
area, or from the California laurel. Because they require a lot
of simmering before their flavor permeates food, they should
be added early on in cooking. The leaves hold their shape
and texture and do not disintegrate during the cooking
process and should always be removed before serving.

SPINACH WITH CHICK PEAS

Chick peas, also known as garbanzo beans,
add a special texture to this lovely
side dish. This can be prepared ahead
and frozen to save time.

INGREDIENTS:

10 ounces fresh
spinach leaves
2 15 ounce cans chick peas
(garbanzo beans), rinsed drained
1 teaspoon cumin seeds
1 small dried red chile,
crushed
10 whole black peppercorns
1 tablespoon red wine vinegar
1/2 cup olive oil
1 2 inch slice bread,
trimmed
4 large cloves garlic,
1 tablespoon paprika
1/2 cup water

Grind cumin, chile and peppercorns in a spice grinder
Set aside. Heat oil in a large pan over medium
high heat. Add bread and 2 cloves garlic and
brown bread on both sides. Transfer garlic
and bread to food processor. Add cumin,
chili and peppercorn to mixture and blend well. Do
not rinse skillet. Place skillet over high heat. Add remaining
garlic cloves and paprika. Stir for 1 minute. Add 1/2 cup water
and wine vinegar to skillet and bring to boil, stirring often. Add
the food processor contents, chick peas and spinach leaves
to skillet. Cook on medium for 10 minutes, until spinach is
tender and mixture starts to thicken. Discard garlic.
Serves 4.

BACON AND HOMINY CASSEROLE

INGREDIENTS:

1/2 pound bacon, sliced
2 15 oz cans hominy, drained
1 green pepper, chopped
1 small onion, chopped
1 16 oz can tomatoes,
undrained
1 tablespoon sugar
1 tablespoon paprika
1/2 cup water

Fry bacon in a skillet. Drain, reserving 2 tablespoons drippings in skillet. Add green pepper and onion. Cook until tender. Add tomatoes with liquid, sugar and salt. Simmer for 10 minutes. Place in a greased baking dish. Crumble bacon over the top and mix with hominy. Pour tomato mixture over top. Bake at 325°F for 45 minutes.
Serves 8.

❖ ❖ ❖ ❖ ❖

CREAMED CORN
WITH CHILES

INGREDIENTS:

7 cups corn, fresh or frozen
4 poblano chiles, sliced
3/4 cup Swiss cheese, cubed
1 onion, chopped
1 clove garlic, minced
4 tablespoons butter
Salt and pepper

Heat butter and sauté chopped onion and garlic until tender. Add corn, poblano chile, Swiss cheese and salt and pepper to taste. Cook over low heat, stirring often, for 30 minutes.
Serves 4.

CREAMED ONIONS

This smooth tasting dish is quickly prepared
and makes a satisfying side to any meal.

INGREDIENTS:

1 1/2 pounds small
white onions
2 tablespoons butter
2 tablespoons flour
1/2 teaspoon salt
1/8 teaspoon pepper
1 1/2 cups half-and-half
1 1/2 cups shredded carrots

Peel onions. In a medium saucepan, bring to a
boil several inches of salted water. Add onions and cover.
Let simmer until onions become tender, about 20 to 30
minutes. Drain. Melt butter over low heat and add flour,
salt and pepper. Cook on low, stirring until mixture is
smooth and bubbly. Remove from heat. Add half-and-half
and bring to a boil, stirring constantly. Boil for 1 minute,
stirring constantly, then add carrots and cook for 5 minutes.
Pour sauce over warm onions.
Serves 6.

NOPALES

Nopales, the leaves of the nopal cactus, have a tart flavor
similar to green pepper and can be found canned or
fresh in most Mexican stores.

HOW TO PREPARE NOPALES:

When preparing fresh nopales, carefully cut off all needles, using
gloves and tongs. When needles have been removed, peel and
dice and cook in hot oil with onion to flavor. Or, cook with hot
chile sauce and onions and season with salt and pepper to taste.

SPANISH RICE

Using chicken or beef broth, instead of water, deepens
the flavor of this very traditional Mexican side dish.

INGREDIENTS:

1 cup
white rice, rinsed
4 cups chicken or
beef broth,
or water
1 small onion, diced
2 tablespoons oil
1/2 cup canned
mixed vegetables, cooked
1/2 cup tomato sauce
1 teaspoon salt
1 teaspoon pepper

Sauté onion in oil and add the rice. Stir constantly over a low
heat until the rice starts to brown. Add tomato sauce, salt
and pepper and liquid. Bring to a boil. Cover pot tightly
and reduce heat, cooking for 15 minutes without removing
the cover. Add the vegetables and cook until the rice is tender.
Serves 4.

CHILI VINEGAR

INGREDIENTS:

12 chiles, red or green,
charred and seeded
6 cups white distilled vinegar

Quarter prepared chiles before bringing vinegar to a boil.
Add chiles and boil mixture for 3 minutes. Set aside to cool
slightly and pour chiles and vinegar into a large jar. Cover tightly
and let sit for 6 weeks. Strain the mixture into 3 or 4
smaller jars and cover tightly.

SAGUARO SQUASH

Here's a way to get your children to love squash. Of course,
with the luscious syrup this could almost be dessert!

INGREDIENTS:

1 4 to 6 pound banana squash
1 pound brown sugar
1/4 cup water
1/2 teaspoon vanilla

Clean the outside of the squash by rinsing with warm water and
toweling dry. Cut squash into quarters and remove seeds. Tightly
pack brown sugar on top of each piece of squash. Put in a pan and
pour the combined water and vanilla over all. Cover tightly and
cook over medium heat until the squash becomes tender. Place
each section in a bowl and pour syrup over the top.
Serves 2.

CARAMEL GLAZED CARROTS

INGREDIENTS:

10 carrots,
peeled and cut in strips
1 cup beef broth
1 1/4 cups packed brown sugar
1 tablespoon Madeira
Water
Salt

Place carrots in a medium saucepan and add water to cover.
Add a dash of salt to water and bring to a boil for 20 to 25
minutes. Set aside. Mix beef broth, brown sugar and wine
in a medium saucepan and stir until sugar dissolves and
mixture coats spoon. Add carrots and cook for 5 minutes.
Serve carrots and spoon caramel mixture over top.
Serves 4.

RICE VERDE

With very little time and effort, a bright and savory side
dish is created. Serve with a side of black beans
for a contrasting effect.

INGREDIENTS:

1/2 cup instant rice
1/2 cup chicken broth
1 large green pepper,
cleaned and seeded
1/2 medium onion
2 cloves garlic
1/4 cup fresh parsley
3 tablespoons oil
Salt
Pepper

Finely chop green pepper, onion, garlic and parsley in a
blender or food processor. In a small pan, heat 1 tablespoon
oil and add green pepper mixture. Cook for 3 minutes,
stirring. Heat 2 tablespoons oil in a large pot and add rice.
Cook over medium heat until lightly browned, stirring often.
Stir in green pepper mixture, broth and salt. Simmer, covered,
until most of the liquid is absorbed. Reduce heat to low and
steam for 15 to 30 minutes. Rice is done when tender.
Salt and pepper to taste.
Serves 6

❖ ❖ ❖ ❖ ❖

A WORD ABOUT CORN:

The history of the Southwest reflects the ancient Indians
belief that man was created from corn by the gods. Today,
corn is still considered an important crop and is the
main ingredient in many recipes, from basic meals
to desserts and beverages.

❖ ❖ ❖ ❖ ❖

LENTILS WITH FRUIT

Topping this dish with slices of pineapple and banana
gives a sweet, fruity flavor to this lentil dish.

INGREDIENTS:

3 slices of bacon,
cut in pieces
1 medium onion,
chopped
1 pound lentils
2 quarts water
1/2 cup
tomato sauce
Salt
Pepper
Sliced bananas
Sliced pineapple

Fry bacon and onion, and add lentils, water and tomato
sauce and salt and pepper to taste. Simmer over medium
heat until lentils are tender and liquid thickens,
approximately 2 hours. Serve with sliced
bananas and pineapple.

A WORD ABOUT MARJORAM

Marjoram is a native of the Mediterranean region and
in the Middle Ages was used for medicinal purposes.
Marjoram, an aromatic member of the mint family
is available as dried leaves or ground.

One half teaspoon oregano leaves
equals the flavor of
one teaspoon marjoram leaves.

GREEN BEAN SALAD

Serve as a cool complement to grilled meats.

INGREDIENTS:

1 pound fresh green beans
1/3 cup olive oil
2 tablespoons lemon juice
Boiling salted water
2 cups water
1/2 medium red onion,
sliced thin
1/2 teaspoon oregano
Salt and pepper.

Wash green beans and snap off tips.
Cut beans in diagonal slices. Cook beans in boiling
salted water for 8 minutes, or until tender. Pour beans
into a sieve and rinse well in cold water. Drain. Beat olive
oil and lemon juice in a small bowl and pour over beans.
Add salt and pepper to taste. Toss well. Bring 2 cups water
to a boil in a small pan. Slide sliced onions into water and
stir. Drain immediately. Place onion slices over beans.

APRICOT VINEGAR

Flavored vinegars add an extra dimension to sauces
and dressings. This Apricot Vinegar is especially tasty!

INGREDIENTS:

1 cup dried apricots
1 quart red wine vinegar

In a stainless steel pan, warm vinegar before pouring
over apricots that have been placed in a sterilized jar.
Seal tightly and let sit for 4 to 6 weeks. Remove apricots
before using. Keep in a sterilized jar or bottle.

RED RICE

A popular addition to many Mexican meals, this rice
dish is easy to prepare and tastes great.

INGREDIENTS:

1 1/2 cups instant rice
1 1/2 cups chicken broth
1 clove garlic, pressed
3 tablespoons oil
1 8 oz can tomato sauce
1/2 medium onion,
chopped

Mix garlic with salt to make a paste. In a large pot, heat
oil and add rice. Cook over medium heat until lightly
browned. Add garlic paste and onion and cook until onion
is tender. Stir in chicken broth and tomato sauce. Cover
and simmer until much of the liquid is absorbed.
Steam on very low heat for 30 to 45 minutes
until rice is tender.
Serves 6.

TOMATO-BROCCOLI SALAD

INGREDIENTS:

2 tomatoes,
cut into wedges
1 1/2 cups broccoli,
cut in bite sized pieces
1/2 head iceberg lettuce
Salad dressing of your choice

Shred lettuce and place on plates. Arrange tomato
wedges and broccoli bits on lettuce and serve
with your favorite dressing.
Serves 4.

RED RICE
AND SHRIMP

In a hurry but want to make something special?
This is the best recipe to use. In this case,
an hour to spend can bring perfection.

INGREDIENTS:

1 pound
shelled green shrimp
1/2 cup onion,
chopped
1 clove garlic,
minced
1 green pepper,
seeded and sliced
1 6 oz can tomato paste
1/4 teaspoon marjoram
1 cup uncooked rice
2 1/2 cups water
1/4 cup oil
Salt
Pepper

Sauté onion and garlic in oil until tender, about 5 minutes.
Add green pepper and uncooked shrimp and cook until
shrimp turn pink. Add tomato paste, water, marjoram
and salt and pepper to taste. Bring to a boil and add
rice, mixing well. Simmer, covered, on low heat for
20 to 30 minutes, until all liquid is absorbed by rice.
Serves 6.

A WORD ABOUT SPICES

Cumin, a native to the Mediterranean region, is
a principal ingredient in Curry Powder and Chili Powder
and is often used in Mexican dishes such
as tamales and chilis.

WHITE RICE AND ARTICHOKES

This unique side dish is an excellent accompaniment
to baked or grilled chicken.

INGREDIENTS:

2 cups rice,
uncooked
1/4 cup olive oil
1 large onion,
diced
5 cups chicken broth
1 cup peas,
fresh or frozen
12 artichoke hearts,
cooked
2 cloves garlic
1 can pimientos,
sliced
Salt
Pepper

Fry rice in oil until it turns light brown. Add onion and
garlic and sauté until onions become tender. Place onion
and garlic in a casserole dish and add boiling broth,
artichokes, peas, pimientos and salt and pepper to taste.
Bake at 350°F until all liquid as been absorbed by
the rice, approximately 35 minutes.
Serves 6.

A WORD ABOUT ONIONS

History tells us that onions have been around
for about 4000 years and were cultivated by
the Babylonians. Members of the lily family,
onions can be used as flakes, powdered, instant
and onion salt.

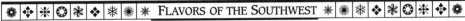
LEEK AND ZUCCHINI FLAN

The subtle flavor of the leek adds a
distinctive flavor to this flan. Garnish
with chopped green onions or
parsley for and extra flair.

INGREDIENTS:

2 leeks, sliced thin
1 pound
zucchini, grated
3 tablespoons
unsalted butter, softened
2 eggs, beaten
1 cup light cream
3 tablespoons
grated Parmesan cheese
1 1/2 teaspoons chervil,
chopped
1 1/2 teaspoons chives,
chopped
Salt
Pepper

Grease 6 soufflé cups and set in a roasting pan.
In a medium sauce pan, cook leeks in boiling salted
water for 6 minutes. Drain and dry with paper towels.
Saute zucchini in butter until tender, about 5 minutes.
Combine zucchini and leeks in mixing bowl. In a separate
bowl, beat eggs, cream, herbs, Parmesan cheese, salt
and pepper until well mixed. Add cream mixture to
zucchini and leeks. Stir. Spoon mixture into soufflé cups,
dividing evenly. Pour boiling water into roasting pan
to halfway up sides of the soufflé cups. Bake
30 to 35 minutes, until flans are firm.
Serves 6.

BREAKFAST
HUEVOS RANCHEROS TO CHORIZO

Many of the busiest people in the Southwest prefer a light meal of fruits and cereal to start their day. However, many of our Hispanic neighbors begin their day with a cup of coffee with milk and a tortilla or piece of bread. This dawn-breaking meal is called *desayuno* in Spanish. Later in the morning a larger meal, *almuerzo*, is served. This meal usually includes beans, tortillas, eggs and chiles and served with coffee. For this chapter we have prepared recipes, both traditional and non-traditional that would be appropriately served for breakfast or as one of many selections offered at a brunch.

* * * * *

HUEVOS RANCHEROS

This is the quintessential Southwestern breakfast.
The reason it's so popular is because it tastes so good!
Serve with warm tortillas.

INGREDIENTS:

4 eggs
1 tablespoon onion, minced
2 tablespoons oil
1/8 teaspoon garlic powder
1 8 ounce can tomato sauce
1 or 2 green chiles, peeled,
mashed and strained
1/2 teaspoon oregano
1 teaspoon salt
1 teaspoon pepper

In a large skillet, sauté onion in oil until tender and add garlic, oregano, green chili, tomato sauce and salt and pepper. Simmer for 5 minutes letting the flavors blend. Poach or fry eggs and cover with sauce. Serve with a side of beans, tortillas and coffee.
Serves 2.

* * * * *

POTATO OLIVE OMELET

Potatoes and olives make an interesting combination.
This omelet is easy to prepare and the green
pepper lends its usual potent flavor.

INGREDIENTS:

1 large potato
6 eggs
2 tablespoons olive oil
1/2 small onion,
chopped
1/4 small green pepper,
diced
3/4 cup Cheddar cheese,
shredded
1/4 cup sliced green olives
1/2 teaspoon oregano
Salt
Pepper

Boil potato in water until tender when pierced with a
fork. When the potato is cool, peel and dice. Saute onion
and bell pepper in 1 tablespoon olive oil until tender.
Mix in potato, olives and oregano and cook until heated
through. Carefully mix in cheese. Salt and pepper to taste.
Cover and set aside. Heat remaining olive oil over
medium-high heat. In another bowl, scramble the eggs.
Add eggs to skillet. Using a spatula, carefully lift edges to
allow uncooked portion of eggs to flow under cooked portion.
Cook eggs just until they set. Spoon filling over half of eggs.
Using a spatula, fold unfilled portion of eggs over filling.
Serves 2.

A WORD ABOUT MARJORAM

One half teaspoon oregano leaves is equal to the flavor
of one teaspoon of marjoram leaves.

* * * * *

FRUIT BOWL

Fruit is nature's candy, and a flavorful snack.
Try this with any selection of fruits, adding wheat
germ or granola cereal for fiber.

INGREDIENTS:

1 ripe papaya,
pitted and sliced
1 pint strawberries,
stemmed and sliced
1 orange,
peeled and sliced
1 red apple,
cored and sliced
1 bunch seedless grapes,
picked from stem
1 1/2 cups low fat plain yogurt
1/4 cup shredded coconut

Mix yogurt with papaya, strawberries, orange slices,
grapes and apple slices. Garnish with shredded coconut and
serve in small bowls. Add your favorite granola if you desire.
Serves 4.

* * * * *

STONED EGGS

INGREDIENTS:

8 eggs, beaten
4 teaspoons butter
16 tablespoons finely
mashed refried beans

To make one omelet at a time; heat 1 teaspoon butter in
heavy skillet. Add enough eggs to make one omelet.
Cook and stir until set. Add 2 tablespoons of beans and stir.
Cook for 1 to 2 minutes.
Serves 4.

* * * * *

EGGS AND SALSA

Fresh salsa really adds a punch to this
egg dish. Serve with refried
beans and corn bread.

INGREDIENTS:

6 eggs
6 corn tortillas
3 tablespoons butter

INGREDIENTS FOR SALSA:

3 large tomatoes
1 4 oz can
green chiles
1 medium onion
1/4 cup fresh cilantro
3 tablespoons lime juice

To prepare salsa; place tomatoes, drained chiles, onion,
cilantro and lime juice in a blender. Blend for 30 seconds,
leaving some texture to salsa. To prepare eggs; place heated
corn tortillas on serving plate, overlapping two per plate.
Fry eggs in butter, two or three at a time. Just before dishing
up, add a small amount of salsa to frying eggs.
Spoon eggs and salsa over waiting corn tortillas.
Serves 3.

A WORD ABOUT OREGANO:

Mexican Oregano grows native over most of New Mexico.
With lavender blossoms and large leaves, this musky flavored
oregano is an authentic flavor of Mexican cooking.
If it is unavailable, it should be left out, not replaced by
the Greek or Italian type of Oregano.

✳ ✳ ✳ ✳ ✳

CHILE AND MUSHROOM OMELET

I was lucky enough to find this recipe
at a quaint Bed and Breakfast in the old mining
town of Bisbee, Arizona.

INGREDIENTS:

8 eggs
3 tablespoons canned
green chiles, diced
1 1/2 tablespoons scallions,
chopped fine
1 cup mushrooms,
sliced thin
4 tablespoons butter
1/4 teaspoon
Tabasco sauce
1/2 cup
Monterey Jack cheese,
shredded
1 tablespoon water
Salt
Pepper

Lightly beat together eggs, diced chiles, scallions,
Tabasco sauce and water. Sauté mushrooms in 2
tablespoons butter until lightly browned. Drain excess
fluid and remove mushrooms. Melt the remaining
2 tablespoons butter in the pan and pour in eggs.
Cook until the omelet starts to set, lifting the edges
to allow liquid to run over the edges. When the
omelet is set, but still moist in the middle,
add mushrooms and cheese evenly over
half, fold to enclose filling. Cook for
2 minutes and serve.
Serves 4.

✳ ✳ ✳ ✳ ✳

CORN SOUFFLE

Even though this souffle is most often eaten
at breakfast, it also makes an excellent
side dish to pork and fish meals.

INGREDIENTS:

1 17 oz can
whole corn
3 eggs,
separated
1/2 medium onion,
chopped fine
3 tablespoons
butter
1/2 cup
chopped green chiles
1/2 teaspoon salt
1/2 teaspoon pepper

Heat oven to 375°F. Prepare a 1 1/2 quart baking
dish by greasing and lightly dusting with flour.
Set aside. In a skillet, sauté onion in butter
until onion becomes tender. Add drained
corn, cooked onion and egg yolks in blender
or food processor. Process until corn is fine.
Pour into a medium bowl. Add chiles and
salt. Stir. In a small bowl beat egg whites
until stiff. Fold gently into corn mixture.
Mix well. Place batter into prepared
baking dish and bake for 10 minutes.
Reduce heat to 350°F and bake
20 to 25 minutes. Soufflé is done
when top begins to brown lightly
and an inserted toothpick
comes out clean.
Serves 6.

✳ ✳ ✳ ✳

SHRIMP STYLE EGGS

This is a sinfully decadent and delectable
breakfast dish that I have found to also be
an especially popular brunch entrée.

INGREDIENTS:

24 small or medium shrimp,
halved horizontally
4 green chiles,
roasted, peeled and seeded
6 tablespoons sour cream,
room temperature
5 tablespoons butter
8 eggs, beaten
8 green onions,
sliced thin
12 corn tortillas
Salt
Pepper

In a skillet, melt butter over medium high heat.
Add shrimp, onions and chiles and sauté until shrimp
turn pink, about 1 minute. Reduce heat to medium
low and add eggs. Gently stir mixture until just set.
Season with salt and pepper and stir in sour cream.
Remove from heat. Using a sharp knife, cut a slit in the
side of each tortilla, forming a pocket. Spoon in the shrimp
and egg mixture, dividing evenly. Transfer to platter.
Garnish with salsa and a dollop of sour cream.
Serves 10.

A WORD ABOUT LITE EATING

Instead of using regular sour cream, substitute with
one of the new low or non-fat sour creams that are
now on the market. The flavor is much the
same with the benefit of being lower in fat.

✳ ✳ ✳ ✳ ✳

CHORIZO

This spicy sausage is used in everything from stews to egg dishes. As well as being a versatile ingredient when cooking, it freezes well, too.

INGREDIENTS:

1/2 pound ground beef
1/2 pound ground pork
1/2 pound ground pork fat
5 dried hot 2 inch chiles
1 teaspoon cumin seed
Oil for frying
1/2 cup
wine vinegar
1/2 teaspoon
garlic powder
1 tablespoon oregano
1 tablespoon paprika
1/2 teaspoon cumin
1/2 teaspoon sugar
1/8 teaspoon cloves,
ground
1 teaspoon salt
1 teaspoon pepper
Sausage casings

Brown chiles and cumin seed in oil, stirring constantly. Drain and cool. Crush chiles. Mix chiles with all other ingredients except sausage casing. Allow flavors to blend by refrigerating in covered bowl for 24 hours. Press chorizo in sausage casings and tie with string every 6 inches. Refrigerate sausages on a rack until dry, at least 1 day, but not longer than 3 days. Cook sausages in a skillet with 4 tablespoons of water. Cover and cook slowly for 10 minutes. Uncover and cook, turning to brown sausages evenly.
Makes 6 long sausages.

✳ ✳ ✳ ✳ ✳

HEARTY CHORIZO EGGS

Hearty is the correct name for this
wonderfully filling breakfast.

INGREDIENTS:

2 large potatoes, peeled
1/2 pound chorizo
1/2 cup onion, chopped fine
1 avocado, sliced
4 eggs

Dice potatoes. Remove casing from chorizo and cook,
scrambled, until brown. Add diced potatoes and onion.
Cover and cook over medium heat for 15 minutes or until
potatoes are tender. Remove cover. Make indentations for
4 eggs in potato mixture. Break an egg and place into each
indentation. Replace cover and cook for 3 to 5 minutes or
until eggs are set. Garnish with avocado slices and serve.
Serves 4.

✳ ✳ ✳ ✳ ✳

SPANISH OMELET

INGREDIENTS:

8 eggs
1 small onion, chopped fine
1 green pepper, chopped fine
3 tablespoons oil
2 8 oz cans tomato sauce
1/2 cup milk
Salt and pepper

Sauté onion and green pepper in hot oil until onion becomes
tender. Add tomato sauce, salt and pepper to taste and simmer
over low heat for 20 minutes. Prepare four separate omelets using
2 eggs and 2 tablespoons milk each. Top omelets with sauce.
Serves 4.

✳ ✳ ✳ ✳ ✳

COTTAGE CHEESE PANCAKES

INGREDIENTS:

1 cup cottage cheese
1/2 cup whole wheat flour
2 teaspoons oil
1/2 teaspoon vanilla
4 eggs

The night before, combine cottage cheese, whole
wheat flour, oil, vanilla and eggs in a blender and blend
until mixed. Refrigerate overnight. When ready to cook,
pour onto heated grill. When tops bubble and bottoms
are brown, flip and cook until light brown on both sides.
Makes 12 pancakes.

✳ ✳ ✳ ✳ ✳

VALLEJO EGGS

INGREDIENTS:

6 eggs
2 canned green chiles,
cut in strips
1/4 cup Monterey Jack cheese,
shredded
1 16 oz can whole tomatoes,
undrained
1 tablespoon butter
1 small onion, sliced
Salt and pepper

Sauté onion slices in butter. Stir in chile strips and tomatoes.
Cook for 4 minutes, cutting tomatoes with a fork. Add salt
and pepper to taste. Break eggs one at a time into a saucer and
slide all eggs at once into the hot tomato sauce. Cover and simmer
for 2 minutes. When eggs are almost set, sprinkle shredded
cheese over eggs. Cook for 3 minutes or until eggs are completely set.
Spoon sauce over eggs as they cook.
Serves 6.

✳ ✳ ✳ ✳ ✳

SUNSHINE SCRAMBLE

INGREDIENTS:

15 large eggs
3 tablespoons oil
1/2 cup jalapeño peppers, diced
1/2 cup red bell pepper, diced
1 small onion, diced
1/4 cup cilantro,
chopped fine
Salt
Pepper

Beat eggs and add jalapeño peppers, red bell pepper, onion,
cilantro and salt and pepper to taste. In a large skillet,
heat oil and add egg mixture. Stir often, scrambling
eggs and cooking evenly.
Serves 6 to 8.

❋ ❋ ❋ ❋ ❋

MEXICAN SCRAMBLED EGGS

INGREDIENTS:

4 eggs
1 tablespoon green
pepper, diced
1 medium tomato
2 teaspoons milk
1 tablespoon parsley, diced
1 small green onion, diced
Salt
Pepper

Peel and cut tomato into squares, removing seeds. Beat
eggs and add milk, tomato, parsley, green pepper,
onion and salt and pepper to taste. Scramble in
butter and serve with warm tortillas.
Serves 2.

❋ ❋ ❋ ❋ ❋

SUNNY BREAKFAST JUICE

You can start your day with extra enthusiasm
by drinking this high energy breakfast drink.

INGREDIENTS:

1 banana, peeled
1 egg (optional)
1 cup orange juice
1 tablespoon wheat germ
1/4 cup nonfat powdered milk
4 or 5 strawberries

Put banana, egg, orange juice, wheat germ, powdered
milk and strawberries into a blender and whirl until smooth.
Pour into large glass and enjoy!
Makes 2 cups.

✳ ✳ ✳ ✳ ✳

TRAILCAKES

INGREDIENTS:

1 cup pancake mix
1 tablespoon oil
1 cup milk
1 egg
1/3 cup Quaker
100% Natural Cereal
1/2 teaspoon sugar

Preheat pan or griddle. Combine pancake mix, oil, milk,
egg and sugar. Stir until smooth and add cereal. Pour mixture,
in desired amounts, on preheated pan or griddle. When cakes
bubble on top, and bottoms are golden brown, turn pancake
and cook other side. Serve with syrup or preserves.
Serves 4.

✳ ✳ ✳ ✳ ✳

DESSERTS
SANTA FE HORNS TO YAM FLAN

Now we come to the best part of any meal, the **dessert**!
Along with some personal favorites such as *Dee Linda's
Cherry Cobbler,* a family recipe, and *Chaco Chocolate
Cake*, I have also included desserts with a uniquely
Southwestern flair, such as *Apple Chili Pie*
and *Yam Flan*. I am sure the following recipes
will touch your sweet tooth in one way or another.

❋ ❋ ❋ ❋ ❋

APPLE-CHILI PIE

This recipe combines the all-American dessert with
the flavor of the Southwest. Experiment with the recipe and
add more chili powder if you're brave enough!

INGREDIENTS:

5 cups apples
3 tablespoons butter
1 cup water
1 cup sugar
1 teaspoon cinnamon
1/2 teaspoon nutmeg
1 teaspoon chili powder
Salt
Pie crust
(see recipe page 201)

Prepare pie crust ahead. Preheat oven to 375ºF. Peel and
slice apples. Place apples, water, sugar, cinnamon, nutmeg,
chili powder and a dash of salt in a large saucepan. Cook over
medium heat for 25 minutes. Pour apple mixture into prepared,
uncooked pie crust and top with butter. Top with crust, prick
vents into top crust using a fork and bake for 35 minutes,
top crust should be golden brown.

❋ ❋ ❋ ❋ ❋

DEE LINDA'S CHERRY COBBLER

My sister, Dee Linda, is as famous for her storytelling
skills as she is for her simply delicious recipes.

INGREDIENTS:

1 cup uncooked oatmeal
1 cup flour
1/4 teaspoon salt
1 cup brown sugar,
firmly packed
1/2 cup butter
1 21 oz can cherry pie filling

Preheat oven to 350°F. Mix oatmeal, flour, salt and
brown sugar. Cut in butter until crumbly. Place half
of the mixture into a well greased 8x8 inch pan.
Layer with pie filling and spread remaining oat mixture
over cherry filling. Bake for 45 minutes and serve hot.

FLAN

INGREDIENTS:

8 eggs
1 3/4 cups sugar
2 teaspoons vanilla
2 large cans evaporated milk

Melt 1 cup sugar in deep pan, stirring constantly until
sugar turns golden. Coat the bottom of the pan with
carmel and cool. Beat eggs, add vanilla remaining sugar
and milk, mixing well. Strain mixture into the pan with
carmel and cover. Place pan into a larger pot containing
hot water. Bake custard at 350°F for 45 minutes to 1 hour,
or until a knife inserted in the center of the custard comes
out clean. Chill for several hours and turn out on a platter.
Serves 8.

SANTA FE HORNS

This lovely dessert is turning up in many of the
finest restaurants across the Southwest.

INGREDIENTS FOR CRUST:

1 cup sugar
3/4 cup blanched almonds
1/4 cup water

INGREDIENTS FOR FILLING:

Vanilla ice cream
Mandarin orange slices
1 pint raspberries
1 pint blackberries

INGREDIENTS FOR SAUCE:

2 cups milk
1/2 cup sugar
1/4 cup flour
4 egg yolks, beaten
1 teaspoon vanilla

Preheat oven to 375°F. Grind sugar and almonds in a blender
until very fine. Add water and blend until mixture becomes a
paste. Let sit for 10 minutes. Place parchment paper over cookie
sheet and spoon 1 inch balls of dough, leaving 4 inches in between
each cookie. Bake in top half of oven for about 12 minutes, until
evenly browned. Use scissors to cut paper between cookies and
quickly fold edges of the paper, pulling each cookie into a horn
shape. Let cool. Work quickly because once cookies cool they
cannot be reshaped. To prepare custard sauce; scald milk and set
aside. Using the top of a double boiler over hot water, blend sugar,
flour and egg yolks. Mix well. Add scalded milk very slowly.
Blend well. Cook, stirring constantly, until it begins to boil and
can coat a spoon. Remove from heat and add vanilla. Stir well.
Once cookies have cooled, fill with softened vanilla ice cream.
Spoon vanilla sauce around filled cookie and add fruit.
Makes 8 horns.

❀ ❀ ❀ ❀ ❀

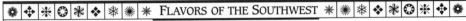
MOCHA CHERRY COOKIES

These tasty tid-bits are the perfect afternoon snack.
Serve with a cup of coffee or cold glass of milk.

INGREDIENTS:

2 cups flour
1/2 cup sugar
2 teaspoons vanilla
1/4 cup unsweetened cocoa
1 tablespoon instant coffee
1 cup walnuts, chopped
1 cup butter, at room temperature
1/2 cup maraschino cherries, diced
1/2 teaspoon salt
Powdered sugar

Preheat oven to 325°F. Blend butter, sugar and vanilla
until fluffy. Sift together cocoa, flour, instant coffee and
salt. Add dry ingredients to butter mixture in small
amounts until combined. Add nuts and cherries and chill.
Using a teaspoon, shape dough into balls and place on a
greased cookie sheet. Bake for 14 to 18 minutes. Sprinkle
with powdered sugar while warm. These are easily frozen.
Makes 6 dozen.

TEQUILA PINEAPPLE

INGREDIENTS:

8 slices of pineapple
1/2 cup sugar
4 ozs white Tequila
1 quart vanilla ice cream

Dredge pineapple slices through the sugar and place in a pan
over heat. Cook pineapple until golden brown on both sides.
Ignite the tequila and pour on the pineapple. Boil for a
few minutes. Serve over ice cream.

SQUASH PIE

The spices in this pie give it the rich, sweet flavor of the
Southwest. Garnish with a lovely hibiscus
blossom to add a touch of elegance.

INGREDIENTS:

1 pound yellow squash
1/4 cup honey
1 tablespoon molasses
1/4 teaspoon ginger
1/2 teaspoon allspice
2 teaspoons cinnamon
2 eggs

Preheat oven to 325°F. Steam squash until it becomes
tender. Cool before cutting in half. Place squash halves
in a blender with honey, molasses, ginger, allspice,
cinnamon and eggs. Blend well. Turn into large baking
pan (more than one may be needed). Bake for 1 hour.
Serves 12.

GRANOLA BARS

INGREDIENTS:

1/2 cup butter
2/3 cup peanut butter
1/3 cup honey
1/2 cup coconut
1/2 cup Grapenut Cereal
2 1/2 cups oatmeal

Preheat oven to 350°F. Combine butter, peanut butter
and honey in a saucepan. Cook over very low heat
until melted. Add coconut, Grapenut Cereal and oatmeal. Mix
well and turn into a glass baking dish. Bake for 18 minutes and
cut into squares. Cool before serving.

FRITTERS

In Mexico fritters are often eaten as an early morning
breakfast along with coffee or a glass of milk. Fritters can also
be served as a snack or as an after dinner treat.

INGREDIENTS:

1/2 cup sugar
1/4 teaspoon salt
1 cup water
4 3/4 cups flour, sifted
2 eggs
3 tablespoons rum
Oil for frying

INGREDIENTS FOR COATING:

1 teaspoon cinnamon
1/2 cup sugar

Mix flour, 1/2 cup sugar and salt in large bowl.
Beat eggs, water and rum together and add to flour
mixture. Mix to form a stiff dough. Place dough on
floured board and knead for 2 minutes until smooth.
Cut dough into 4 sections. Roll sections on floured pastry
cloth until there are 4 rectangles 10x15 inches. Cut into
2x5 inch strips. Twist two strips of dough together to form
fritters. Heat oil to 370°F in a skillet. Mix 1/2 cup sugar and
cinnamon together in a shallow pan and set aside. Fry dough
until golden and place on paper towel to drain excess liquid.
Dip in cinnamon sugar and coat.
Makes 40.

A WORD ABOUT CINNAMON:

Cinnamon, considered the best known of all spices
and the most important spice used for baking, is the inner
bark of the evergreen tree, a member of the laurel family.

❋ ❋ ❋ ❋ ❋

PRICKLY PEAR SORBET

When picking fruit from the Prickly Pear Cactus,
choose the darkest fruit for the richest flavor.

INGREDIENTS:

8 prickly pear fruit,
peeled
6 tablespoons sugar
Juice from 1/2 lemon

In a blender, blend fruit then strain. Add sugar and lemon
juice and place in an ice cream maker. Follow
manufacturer's instructions to make ice cream.
Garnish with a sprig of mint.
Serves 4.

LEMON-PINEAPPLE MOUSSE

INGREDIENTS:

1 box lemon gelatin
2 cups boiling water
1 pint
pineapple sherbet
1 1/2 tbsp lemon juice
3 tablespoons
lemon rind, grated

Mix gelatin into boiling water. Add sherbet, lemon juice
and 1 tablespoon lemon rind. Using an electric mixer,
beat on low until sherbet melts. Pour into 6 dessert
dishes and chill until set.
Garnish with remaining lemon rind.
Serves 6.

CHACO CHOCOLATE CAKE

I'm not sure if the Chaco Culture Indians of
New Mexico really had a recipe like this.
If they had, they would probably still
be hanging around today!

INGREDIENTS FOR CAKE:

1/2 cup butter, softened
1 1/2 cups sugar
2 eggs
2 cups flour, sifted
1/2 teaspoon salt
1 cup sour milk
3 squares Hershey's Baking
Chocolate, melted
1 teaspoon baking soda
1 tablespoon vinegar

INGREDIENTS FOR FROSTING:

3/4 cup butter,
softened
3 cups powdered sugar
1/2 cup cocoa
1/2 teaspoon vanilla
1/4 cup milk

To prepare cake; preheat oven to 375°F. Combine sugar
and butter, creaming them together. Add 1 egg and
beat well. Add remaining egg and beat well. Stir in flour
and salt and add, alternately, with milk, beating well.
Dissolve baking soda in vinegar and add to cake mixture
with melted chocolate, mixing well. Grease 9-inch cake pans
and pour cake mixture into pans. Bake for 25 minutes and
set aside to cool. To prepare frosting; cream butter with one
cup sugar. Add remaining sugar, cocoa, vanilla and milk.
Beat until smooth. When cake has completely cooled, spread
frosting over top of the bottom layer before topping with
second layer of cake. Finish cake by frosting top and sides.
Serves 8.

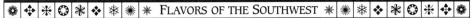
PUMPKIN SQUARES

Here's a new twist to an American tradition.
The pecan topping gives it an extra sweet touch.

INGREDIENTS FOR CRUST:

1/2 cup oatmeal
1 cup flour
1/2 cup
butter, melted
1/2 cup
brown sugar

INGREDIENTS FOR FILLING:

1 16 ounce
can pumpkin
1 large can
evaporated milk
3/4 cup sugar
2 eggs
1 1/2 teaspoons
cinnamon
1/4 teaspoon
ground cloves

INGREDIENTS FOR TOPPING:

2 tablespoons
butter, softened
1/2 cup chopped pecans
1/2 cup brown sugar

To prepare crust; preheat oven to 350°F. Combine oatmeal,
flour, butter and brown sugar. Press into a 9x13 inch pan.
Bake for 15 minutes. To prepare filling; combine pumpkin,
evaporated milk, sugar, eggs, cinnamon and cloves.
Mix well and pour into baked crust. Bake for 20 minutes.
To prepare topping; mix pecans, brown sugar and butter.
Sprinkle over top of pie. Bake for 20 more minutes.
Cool before cutting into squares.

MEXICAN WEDDING CAKES

This Mexican sweet reflects the joy and happiness
in the celebrations of life. This is baked not
only for weddings, but all year round.

INGREDIENTS:

1 cup butter
1/3 cup sugar
2 1/2 cups flour, sifted
1 teaspoon almond flavoring
1 cup pecans, chopped fine
Red food coloring
Green food coloring
Salt

Blend butter and sugar in bowl until smooth.
Add almond flavoring and stir. Add flour, nuts and dash of
salt and mix well. Separate dough into halves and add three
or four drops of green food coloring to one half and red to
the other half. Chill all dough for 3 hours. Form small balls with
dough and place on greased cookie sheet. Use a covered glass
bottom to flatten each ball to 1/4 inch thickness. Preheat oven
to 375°F and cook for 12 to 15 minutes, or until edge of
cookies turn light brown.
Makes 36.

A WORD ABOUT DESSERTS:

Mexicans are known for having a sweet tooth and
Mexican cooks always serve their family and guests
some sort of after meal sweet. Sometimes this will consist of
a simple bowl of fruit with sweet cream. Often something
a little more elaborate, such as the ever popular flan
or a delectable bread pudding is served.

BANANAS WITH RUM

INGREDIENTS:

6 ripe bananas,
1 teaspoon vanilla extract
1 cup almonds, chopped
1 cup raisins
1/2 stick butter
1/2 cup brown sugar
2 tablespoons rum
1 cup whipped cream

Mix vanilla, almonds and raisins. Set aside. Heat butter
and sugar over medium heat until melted. Add sliced
bananas and cook until tender. Remove from heat and
add rum, stirring gently. Top with whipped cream.

SWEET POTATO PUDDING

INGREDIENTS:

2 cups sweet potato,
cooked and mashed
1 cup crushed pineapple
1 teaspoon cinnamon
1/2 teaspoon ground cloves
1/4 teaspoon salt
3/4 cup ground almonds
1 cup sugar
Whipped cream

Combine sweet potato, sugar, pineapple, cinnamon,
cloves, almonds and salt, mix well. Cook over low heat,
stirring often. When the mixture looses its shine and
becomes a mass, move to a serving dish and garnish
with whipped cream. Serve hot or cold.
Serves 6.

❀ ❀ ❀ ❀ ❀

KINGS BREAD RING

In Mexico the Kings Bread Ring is traditionally served on All Kings' Day, January 6. The person who finds the hidden coin in their serving must host a party on February 2.

INGREDIENTS:

4 1/2 cups all purpose flour
2 packages dry yeast
1 1/2 teaspoons orange peel, grated
1/4 cup butter, melted
1 cup warm milk
1/3 cup butter
1/3 cup sugar
3 eggs, beaten
2 teaspoons salt

INGREDIENTS FOR ICING:

1 to 2 tablespoons milk
1 1/3 cups powdered sugar
1 teaspoon rum flavoring
7 candied cherries, chopped
10 candied orange peel strips,
2 to 3 inches long

Dissolve yeast into milk by stirring. Cream sugar and 1/3 cup butter. Blend in salt and orange peel. Add yeast mixture, 1 egg and enough flour to make the dough stiff. Place dough on a lightly floured surface and knead until smooth and elastic, approximately 10 minutes. Put dough in greased bowl and grease top. Cover dough and let rise until it doubles in size. Punch down. Knead until smooth, about 2 minutes. Roll dough into long strand and place on greased baking sheet. Shape into ring and seal ends together. Take a coin and push it into dough, making sure to cover it completely. Brush lightly with melted butter and cover. Let rise until it doubles, approximately 1 1/2 hours. Bake at 375°F for 30 minutes or until golden. While bread is cooling, combine powdered sugar, milk and rum flavoring. Beat until smooth and frost cooled bread. Decorate with candied fruit. Serves 12.

LEMON ICE

A delightful finish to any meal, satisfying
without being too sweet.

INGREDIENTS:

3/4 cup lemon
juice, fresh is best
3 1/2 cups water
1 1/2 cups sugar
2 tablespoons lemon zest
1 lemon, sliced thin

Bring water to a boil in a saucepan and add sugar,
stirring until dissolved. Remove from heat and let cool.
Add lemon juice and zest. When lemon mixture has cooled,
pour into an ice cream maker and follow the manufacturers
instructions for making ice cream. Garnish with lemon slices
and serve in decorative ice cream dishes or cocktail glasses.
Serves 6.

PICACHO PEAK PINEAPPLE PLEASURE

INGREDIENTS:

1 large pineapple
2/3 cup sour cream
2 tablespoons sugar
1 tablespoon
packed brown sugar
1/2 cup pecans, chopped

Slice 1/3 off the side of a pineapple, leaving the crown.
Use a grapefruit knife to remove fruit to 1/2 inch of the shell.
Remove fruit, discarding core, and cut into bite sized pieces.
Sprinkle sugar over pineapple pieces and return to the
pineapple shell. Mix sour cream and brown sugar then spoon
over pineapple. Garnish with chopped pecans and serve.
Serves 6.

YAM FLAN

A Southwest version of the more traditional Mexican Flan,
this yummy creation is colorful and tastes divine.

INGREDIENTS:

1 1/2 pounds
yams, about 3 yams
1 1/2 cups sugar
3/4 cup water
8 eggs
2 egg yolks
1 14 ounce can
sweetened condensed milk
1 cup half and half
1 cup heavy cream
1 1/4 teaspoons vanilla
1/2 teaspoon cinnamon
1/2 teaspoon nutmeg
1/2 teaspoon allspice

Clean yams and bake at 325ºF for about 1 1/2 hours.
When yams have been cooked until soft, peel and purée.
There should be 1 1/2 cups puréed yams. Set aside. Prepare
caramel by bringing sugar and 1/4 cup water to a boil in a
large saucepan. Do not stir. When syrup becomes lightly
brown and bubbles, pour syrup into a 9 inch glass flan
pan or dish, turning dish until syrup covers the entire bottom
and some of the sides. Pour excess syrup back into pot and
add remaining 1/2 cup water and bring to a boil. This thinner
syrup will be served with flan. Set aside. Combine eggs and egg
yolks and beat until fluffy. Add condensed milk, half and half,
vanilla, cinnamon, nutmeg, allspice and puréed yams and beat
well. Pour mixture into the prepared dish and set inside a roasting
pan. Pour boiling water into roasting pan until water comes half
way up side of flan dish. Bake until flan is firm, about 1 hour.
Take flan dish out of water and cool to room temperature before
refrigerating. Remove flan by sliding a moistened knife around
edge of dish. Place serving plate over top of flan and flip over,
flan should slide out easily. Serve with remaining syrup.

NANNA'S APRICOT PIE

My grandmother, Mary V. Barker, was the creator of this very flavorful sweet and sour pie. Use only name brand dried apricots for the tartest taste.

INGREDIENTS FOR CRUST:

2 cups sifted flour
1 teaspoon salt
2/3 cup shortening
4 teaspoons butter
1/2 cup ice water

INGREDIENTS FOR FILLING:

2 bags dried apricots
2 1/2 cups sugar
1/2 teaspoon nutmeg
1/2 teaspoon cinnamon
Water

To prepare crust; combine flour and salt, add shortening and butter, cutting into flour with a knife. When mixture consists of pebble sized lumps add ice water, a little at a time, until dough forms a ball. Cover with plastic and chill for 1/2 hour. Roll out dough on a lightly floured board. Preheat oven to 425°F. To prepare filling; place apricots in medium bowl and cover with water. Add sugar, nutmeg and cinnamon. Microwave until apricots become tender, but not mushy, 40 to 50 minutes. Pour filling into uncooked pie crust and cover with top crust, pricking with a fork in an attractive design to allow steam to vent. Bake until crust is golden brown, 25 to 30 minutes. Serve with vanilla ice cream. Serves 6.

CRÉME BRULÉE

Many of the better restaurants here in the Southwest offer this elegant creation on their dessert menus. The addition of raspberries or sliced strawberries to the custard just before refrigerating will add a special taste treat.

INGREDIENTS:

2 cups heavy cream
1 vanilla bean,
split
4 egg yolks
5 tablespoons sugar

Preheat oven to 325°F. In the top of a double boiler, pour cream and add vanilla bean. Cover and cook over boiling water until a wrinkled skin develops over surface, scalding point. In a separate bowl, beat egg yolks and 1 tablespoon sugar until light in color. Remove vanilla bean from cream and pour cream into egg yolk mixture very slowly, stirring constantly. Return mixture to pan and cook over boiling water, stirring constantly, until custard thickens enough to coat a wooden spoon. Make sure the mixture never comes to a boil, or it will curdle. Strain custard into a shallow baking dish and bake for 5 to 8 minutes. When a skin forms on top, remove from oven and refrigerate for 3 to 4 hours, or overnight. Preheat broiler. Sprinkle top of cold crème with 4 tablespoons sugar and place under a heated broiler, 4 inches from broiler. Make sure broiler is very hot to prevent custard from bubbling through sugar topping. If this starts to happen, remove dish at once or custard will burn. When crème is complete, refrigerate for 2 to 3 hours before serving.
Serves 6.

OATMEAL AND ALMOND COOKIES

These tasty cookies are a favorite of children all over the Southwest. Make a double batch and freeze.

INGREDIENTS:

1/2 cup sugar
1/2 cup brown sugar,
packed
1/2 cup butter,
softened
1/2 teaspoon vanilla
1 egg
1 1/2 cups
fast cooking oats
1/2 cup flour
1/2 cup toasted almonds,
ground
1/2 teaspoon baking soda
1/4 teaspoon baking powder
1/8 teaspoon salt
1/2 cup almonds,
sliced

Preheat oven to 375°F. Combine sugar, brown sugar, butter, vanilla and egg. Mix well. Add oats, flour, ground almonds, baking soda, baking powder and salt, mixing well. Add sliced almonds. Place rounded teaspoonfuls of dough onto an ungreased cookie sheet, about 2 inches apart. Bake for 10 minutes, or until golden brown. Cool before removing from cookie sheet.
Makes about 36 cookies.

DRUNKEN PUDDING

The brandy gives it the tipsy name and
your taste buds will be drunk with pleasure
when experiencing this delight.

INGREDIENTS:

10 ladyfingers cookies
1/2 cup brandy
6 egg yolks
1/4 cup sugar
1/4 teaspoon salt
2 cups hot milk
1 teaspoon vanilla
1 cup whipped cream
1 cup almonds,
chopped
Maraschino Cherries

In a medium bowl, break up ladyfingers. Sprinkle with
liquor, set aside. Beat egg yolks with sugar and salt in the
top of a double boiler. Gradually add hot milk to egg mixture.
Cook over simmering water, stirring often, until mixture
coats the back of a spoon. Remove from stove. Add vanilla
and cool. Fold whipped cream and custard into ladyfinger
mixture. Add nuts and chill. Garnish with cherries.
Serves 8.

A WORD ABOUT MEXICAN CREAM:

Crema Natural is a slightly sour cream
that thickens with age.

Crema Dulce is a sweet cream very
similar to our whipping cream.

APPLE BURRITO'S

This dessert is simply divine. The apple-cinnamon filling is tasty enough to make this a prize winning selection.

INGREDIENTS:

8 Granny Smith apples,
sliced
1 cup water
1 cup sugar
1/2 teaspoon cinnamon
1/8 teaspoon nutmeg
12 large flour tortillas
1 cup Cheddar cheese,
shredded

Preheat oven to 350°F. Combine water, sugar, cinnamon and nutmeg and bring to a boil. Add apples and simmer on medium low heat until tender, but still firm. Drain apples, reserving juice. Divide the apple mixture and cheese equally on all tortillas. Spoon 3 teaspoons of syrup over apples and cheese and fold. In a buttered baking dish place filled tortillas, seam side down, and spoon remaining syrup over the top. Bake for 5 to 10 minutes. When tortillas begin to crisp, remove from oven.
Serves 12.

A WORD ABOUT SPICES:

Nutmeg is the oval shaped, dried seed of an evergreen tree with a fruit similar to an apricot. Nutmeg has a sweet and spicy flavor and is often used to season meats, sauces, cookies, pies and other pastries.

BAKED PEACHES

Place baked peaches in an attractive bowl
for an elegant presentation.

INGREDIENTS:

4 large
ripe peaches
1 pound
apricots, pitted
2 cups water
1 1/4 cups
fine sugar
1/4 cup brown
sugar, packed
1/2 cup
chopped pecans
1/2 cup coconut
2 tablespoons butter,
softened

Combine apricots, water and 1 cup fine sugar
in a saucepan. Bring mixture to a boil and
simmer for 7 minutes. Set aside. Blanch peaches
in boiling water for 2 minutes. Dip peaches in
ice cold water which will make removal of the
skin very easy. Cut off the top of the peach at
the pit. Remove pit. Combine brown sugar, pecans,
coconut and 1 tablespoon butter. Fill peaches with pecan
mixture. Grease a baking pan with the remaining butter
and place peaches on pan with apricots surrounding them.
Discard poaching fluid. Top with remaining sugar and bake
for 8 to 10 minutes. Remove peaches to serving dishes
and place baking pan on the stove over medium heat
to reduce juices. Purée apricots in a blender and push
purée through a sieve. Spoon apricot sauce around
peaches and serve while hot. Great with a scoop
of French Vanilla or Peach ice cream. Serves 4.

DESERT DESSERT TAMALES

The date-nut filling makes these tamales a temptingly tasty treat. Make them when you are serving regular tamales as a main course for a very special dessert.

INGREDIENTS:

3 1/2 dozen dry corn husks
4 cups masa harina flour
1 cup lard
1 cup sugar
1 teaspoon salt
1 cup brown sugar
1/2 teaspoon cinnamon
1/4 cup butter
1 cup pitted dates, chopped
1 cup pecans, chopped

In a large saucepan, cover corn husks with boiling water. Soak for at least 30 minutes. Beat lard until fluffy, using mixer. Combine masa flour, sugar and salt. Gradually add the flour and sugar mixture to lard and add water until dough sticks together and has a pastelike consistency. To prepare date filling; blend brown sugar, butter and cinnamon until smooth. Dry husks by placing on paper towels and patting dry. Add chopped dates and pecans and mix evenly. Spread 2 tablespoons tamale dough on center portion of husk, leaving at least a 2 inch margin at both ends and about a 1/2 inch margin at the right side. Spoon 1 1/2 tablespoons filling onto dough. Wrap tamale, overlapping left side first, then right side slightly over left. Fold bottom up and top down. Lay tamales in top section of steamer with open flaps on bottom. Tie with string if husks are too short to stay closed. Tamales may completely fill the top section of steamer but should be placed so there are spaces between them for the circulation of steam. Steam over simmering water for 1 hour, until corn husks can be peeled from dough easily. Makes 3 1/2 dozen tamales.

BEVERAGES
MARGARITAS TO MIMOSAS

One of the basic tenets of Southwestern living is the emphasis on casual simplicity. This is reflected in many of the **beverages** served with foods of the Southwest. Tequila is the perfect example. Originally served in shot glasses, or straight from the bottle, with a wedge of lime and a shaker of salt on the side, until someone simplified things by combining the three, adding a dash of Triple Sec, and pouring it over ice. Variations of this drink, now called *Margaritas*, are being served all over America. The drinks in this chapter compliment the spicy foods served in the Southwest and help douse fires in the mouths of many chile lovers. Sample these drinks to discover which suits you best.

MARGARITA

Legend has it that the Margarita was invented by a bartender in Tijuana, Mexico who named it after a beautiful Hollywood movie star.

INGREDIENTS:

4 ounces tequila
(preferably Cuervo Gold)
2 tablespoons Triple Sec
1/4 cup lime juice
1 lime, sliced
1 1/2 teaspoons sugar
Salt
Crushed Ice

Combine tequila, Triple Sec, lime juice, sugar and crushed ice. Blend on high. Rub a lime slice around the rim of chilled glasses and dip in salt. Pour Margarita mixture into glasses and garnish with slices of lime.

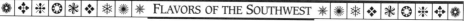

SUN TEA

Arizona boasts over 300 sunny days a year, that
means Sun Tea can be made almost every day!

INGREDIENTS:

1 gallon water
6 single
tea bags

Find a gallon jug or jar and clean thoroughly.
Fill with water and add tea bags. Cover and place
in a sunny spot. When water becomes clear brown,
bring indoors. To avoid clouding, let tea cool to
room temperature before refrigerating. Pour
over ice and add lemon or desired sweetener.
For flavored teas, use flavored tea bags.
Serves many!

❂ ❂ ❂ ❂ ❂

PINEAPPLE PLEASURE

This pineapple drink seems to be exactly the right thing to
serve on those hot summer days playing by the pool.

INGREDIENTS:

1/2 cup canned or fresh
crushed pineapple with juice, frozen
3/4 cup milk (nonfat or regular)
1/4 teaspoon rum flavoring
1/8 teaspoon nutmeg
1/8 teaspoon cinnamon
2 teaspoons sugar

Place frozen crushed pineapple, milk, rum flavoring,
nutmeg, cinnamon and sugar in a blender. Blend on
high until creamy. Pour into chilled glasses and serve.
Serves 2.

❂ ❂ ❂ ❂ ❂

SANGRIA

Not only is this a great drink to serve
at any time, it adds a beautiful touch when
served in a large punch bowl.

INGREDIENTS:

1 bottle dry red wine
1 cup orange juice
1 7 oz bottle club soda
1 lime, sliced
1 orange, sliced
2 cups fresh pineapple,
cubed

Combine wine, lime slices, orange slices and pineapple
cubes and chill. Add club soda before serving and pour over ice.
Serves 6.

❂ ❂ ❂ ❂ ❂

HARD CIDER PUNCH

An excellent selection for entertaining on a cool desert
evening, or during the festive holiday season.

INGREDIENTS:

2 quarts hard cider
6 tablespoons brandy
2 apples, sliced
2 tablespoons sugar
2 oranges,
stuck with 6 cloves each

In a large saucepan, combine cider, brandy, apples,
sugar and cloved oranges. Simmer over medium to low
heat for 25 minutes. Cool before serving from punch bowl.
Serves 10.

❂ ❂ ❂ ❂ ❂

TEQUILA SUNRISE

The Tequila Sunrise is as well known as the Margarita.
Both signify the mellow atmosphere of the Southwest.

INGREDIENTS:

4 ounces tequila
(preferably Cuervo Gold)
1 cup fresh orange juice
2 teaspoons lime juice
2 tablespoons grenadine
Crushed Ice
Maraschino Cherries

Combine tequila, orange juice, lime juice and grenadine
in a blender or shaker. Pour into tall glasses over ice.
Garnish with a cherry.
Serves 2.

MEXICAN PUNCH

This is a fresh and zesty cooler perfect for a fiesta or
pool party when your favorite friends gather together.

INGREDIENTS:

2 ozs cranberry juice
2 ozs grenadine
2 ozs piña colada mix
2 ozs pineapple juice
Splash of 7-Up
Ice

Place cranberry juice, grenadine, piña colada mix and
pineapple juice in a blender. Blend and pour into tall
glasses over ice. Add splash of 7-Up and garnish
with orange slices if desired.
Serves 2.

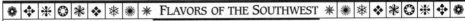

KILLER CRANBERRY COCKTAIL

This fresh tasting drink is dangerous as well as delicious!
Serve in tall, chilled glasses.

INGREDIENTS:

4 ounces cranberry juice
1/2 ounce
Cranberry Schnapps
1 ounce vodka
6 cubes of ice
Lime slices

Combine cranberry juice, Schnapps, vodka and ice
in a blender. Blend until smooth. Pour into chilled
glasses and garnish with lime slices.

✿ ✿ ✿ ✿ ✿

ORANGE SPRITZER

This fruity drink is rich with the citrus flavor of the orange
and lemon juices, but the blended peaches make
this a mouth watering treat.

INGREDIENTS:

2 medium peaches
1 cup fresh orange juice
1/2 cup fresh lemon juice
2 tablespoons sugar
8 ice cubes
Orange slices

Rinse, slice and pit peaches. Place peaches, orange
juice, lemon juice, sugar and ice in a blender and
blend until smooth. Garnish with orange slices.
Serve in tall glasses.
Serves 4.

✿ ✿ ✿ ✿ ✿

MEXICAN HOT CHOCOLATE

If Mexican chocolate is unavailable, use American
sweet chocolate and add a dash of cinnamon.

INGREDIENTS:

4 cups milk
4 oz Mexican chocolate,
grated
1/2 cup cream
2 tablespoons sugar
1/2 teaspoon cinnamon
1 egg yolk

Heat 1 cup milk and add chocolate. Stir until chocolate
melts. Add remaining milk. Mix egg yolk with
cream, add sugar and cinnamon. Combine with hot
milk and simmer, stirring constantly. When hot, remove
from heat and beat with mixer until a layer of
foam coats the top. Serve hot.

STRAWBERRY SIREN

Using fresh strawberries is the secret to this zippy,
frothy drink. If serving to children, omit the
alcohol and blend with ice.

INGREDIENTS:

4 cups fresh strawberries
2 ounces tequila
1 cup water

Gently clean strawberries and remove stems. Place strawberries
in a blender and purée, adding tequila and water. Chill for
at least 1/2 hour. Pour over ice and serve.
Place whole strawberry in glass to garnish.
Serves 4.

ICED COFFEE

With the many flavors of coffee available
these days, you can try a different flavor
every day of the week.

INGREDIENTS:

Pot of your favorite coffee
Cream
Sugar
Ice

Make a pot of your favorite coffee and pour into
tall glasses over ice. Add sugar and cream to taste.
Serves 4 to 6.

❁ ❁ ❁ ❁ ❁

LEMON MIRAGE

Long time residents of Phoenix claim this drink helps
make the summers a little easier to live with.

INGREDIENTS:

1 6 oz can frozen lemonade
1 6 oz can frozen limeade
1 6 oz can frozen orange juice
3 to 4 cups cold water
1 quart 7-Up, cold
1 quart lemon/lime seltzer
Lemon slices
Orange slices

In a large punch bowl combine lemonade, limeade,
orange juice, water, seltzer and 7-Up.
Add lemon and orange slices.
Serves 8.

❁ ❁ ❁ ❁ ❁

SANGRITA

Sangritas are perfect chasers to a shots of Tequila.

INGREDIENTS:

1/2 cup orange juice
2 cups chilled tomato juice
2 jalapeño peppers,
seeded and halved
1/4 cup onion, quartered
1 tablespoon lime juice
2 teaspoons sugar
1/2 teaspoon hot pepper sauce
1/2 teaspoon salt

Combine orange juice, tomato juice, jalapeño peppers,
onion, lime juice, sugar, hot pepper sauce and salt in a
blender. Blend until smooth. Chill before serving.
Serves 4.

SHERBET ACAPULCO

This is a very tasty drink that is great on warm days.
Omit the alcohol when serving to children.

INGREDIENTS:

1 1/2 pints lemon sherbet
1/4 cup lime juice
4 tablespoons rum
5 tablespoons tequila
Peeled orange sections

Soften sherbet and add lime juice, rum and tequila.
Mix well and refreeze. Scoop mixture into individual
glasses and place a fresh orange section in each glass.
Serves 4.

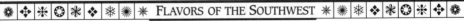
STRAWBERRY SPRITZER

Fresh strawberries are abundant in the Southwest.
This combines fresh and frozen fruit to make
a refreshing beverage.

INGREDIENTS:

1 pint fresh strawberries
3 10 ounce packages
frozen strawberries
28 ounces carbonated water
6 cups white grape juice

Thaw strawberries. Blend 2 packages of strawberries,
with juice, until smooth. Pour into large punch bowl
and add remaining package, with juice. Add grape
juice and carbonated water, stir gently. Garnish
with fresh strawberries.

MIMOSA

A wonderfully refreshing drink at any time,
especially popular at brunch.

INGREDIENTS:

Fresh
orange juice
Champagne
Fresh
Strawberries

Pour orange juice
and add Champagne to taste.
Garnish with fresh strawberries.
Serves many!

OLD FASHIONED LEMONADE

This classic lemonade is made with real lemon juice,
increase or decrease the sugar amount to
suit your own tastes.

INGREDIENTS:

3 cups water
Juice from 4 lemons
1/2 cup sugar
Ice

Combine water, lemon juice and sugar.
Stir until sugar dissolves and pour over ice.
Garnish with a slice of lemon.
Serves 4.

LEMON TEA

Lemon and tea go together like a hug and a squeeze.
Take a moment out of your day and try
this age old favorite.

INGREDIENTS:

4 cups boiling water
6 to 8 tea bags
Juice from 2 lemons
Peel from 1 lemon
1/2 cup sugar
Ice

Pour boiling water over tea bags. Steep to desired
strength and let cool to room temperature. Combine tea,
lemon juice, lemon peel, and sugar and pour
into tall glasses over ice.
Serves 8.

INDEX

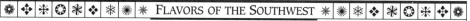